VOCABULARY CARTOONS II

SAT Word Power

Learn Hundreds of SAT Words
Fast with Easy Memory Techniques

Revised & Updated Edition

New Monic Books, Inc.

Manufactured in the United States of America.
Library of Congress Catalog Card Number: 96-96399
ISBN: 10 digit 0-9652422-4-2
ISBN: 13 digit 978-0-9652422-4-0
Illustrations: Joseph Toth, Lee Horton, David Horton, Luke Wilson, & John Telford
Cover Design: Bryan Burchers
Setup & Typography: Bryan Burchers & Sam Burchers III

Library of Congress Cataloging-in-Publication Data
Burchers, Sam
   Vocabulary Cartoons II, SAT Word Power
   Sam Burchers, Jr., Sam Burchers, III & Bryan Burchers
        p.   cm.
   Includes index.
   ISBN 978-0-9652422-4-0
   Vocabulary Cartoons II, SAT Word Power, 2nd Edition

                    96-96399

New Monic Books
P.O. Box 511314
Punta Gorda, FL 33951
(941) 575-6669 $12.95
www.vocabularycartoons.com

Acknowledgments

The Educators

Our gratitude to the following educators in Southwest Florida who had the foresight and initiative to introduce mnemonic cartoon test programs in their schools and classrooms. It was through their efforts that vocabulary cartoons have been proven to be a dynamic new technique in building a more educated vocabulary:

North Fort Myers High School
Ed Stickles, Princ.
Larry Marsh

Cape Coral High School
Karyl Davis, Asst. Princ. Cur.
Melisa Skinner

Murdock Middle School
Lou Long, Princ.
Debbie Moore
William Valella

Alva Middle School
Jerry Demming, Asst. Princ. Cur.
Jean Riner

Port Charlotte Middle School
Clyde Hoff, Princ.
Dianne Woolley

Mariner High School
Bonnie Hill, Asst. Princ. Cur.
Judy Baxley
Jennifer Basler
Sharon Kramer
Nancy Wiseman

The Artists

Our special thanks to staff artists Joe Toth, Gene Ostmark, Bryan Burchers, Lee Horton and Dave Horton, and contributing artists Luke Wilson and John Telford. Their collective talents provided the essential quality of zany humor and outrageous bizarreness that make cartoon mnemonics memorable.

Contents

Introduction

About Vocabulary Cartoons I

First published in 1996, *Vocabulary Cartoons, SAT Word Power* was intended to be our only vocabulary book. Shortly thereafter, teachers began using our book in their classrooms with great success. Educators were impressed with the ease and proficiency with which their students were learning new words. Many were learning two to three times more words than students using traditional rote memory vocabulary books. By 1998 *Vocabulary Cartoons, SAT Word Power* had become Ingram's (the USA's largest retail book distributor) best selling vocabulary book in the nation*. Encouraged with the success of our first book, we set out to write a series of Vocabulary Cartoon books using the same mnemonic format.

Vocabulary Cartoons, Elementary Edition

Due to the demand for a lower level vocabulary book, we published *Vocabulary Cartoons, Elementary Edition* in 1998. Used primarily in 3rd through 6th grades, the *Elementary Edition* soon gained recognition similar to our first book. In addition, middle and high schools soon began using this book with their challenged students. Accordingly, the "Elementary Edition" title was taken off the cover so it could more easily be used in both primary and secondary schools without offending non-elementary students.

*Source: Ingram Book Company

Vocabulary Cartoons II, SAT Word Power

The book you are now reading, *Vocabulary Cartoons II, SAT Word Power*, picks up where SAT I leaves off. It also contains 290 words commonly found in national SAT tests. In verbal difficulty, the words in this edition are equal to the words found in *Vocabulary Cartoons I*.

Brain-Friendly Learning With Vocabulary Mnemonics

In recent years neuroscientists have uncovered astonishing facts about how the brain learns, stores, and retrieves information! The use of mnemonic applications is high on the list of the way the brain learns most naturally and efficiently. Vocabulary Cartoon mnemonic strategies not only accelerate learning, but they also motivate, entertain, and build self-esteem!

Vocabulary Cartoons and How They Work

Vocabulary Cartoons consist of both rhymes and humorous cartoons that employ proven mnemonic techniques into the vocabulary learning experience. All mnemonics are based on association, the idea being to associate what you are trying to remember with something you already know.

Rhymes and Jingles are effective memory aids. Linking rhyming words to words you already know is classic mnemonic methodology. Who in America does not know the date America was discovered by the jingle, "Columbus Sailed The Ocean Blue?"

Visual Images in the form of humorous cartoons make up the second mnemonic. Anything that can be visualized is easier to remember. The more bizarre or outrageous the cartoon, the easier it is to remember.

Who Would Most Benefit From This Book?

Vocabulary Cartoons and *Vocabulary Cartoons II* are designed for anyone wishing to build a stronger vocabulary. However, they are particularly recommended for students studying for Pre-Scholastic Aptitude Tests (PSAT), Scholastic Aptitude Tests (SAT) and Graduate Record Exams (GRE); they are also suitable for older students in Adult Education courses, English as a Second Language (ESOL) students; those in Exceptional Student Education (ESE) programs and Attention Deficit Disorder (ADD) programs.

School Test Results

The effectiveness of *Vocabulary Cartoons* as a faster, easier learning tool for all types of students has been established in six independent school tests in Southwest Florida. These tests took place in 1995 and 1996 and involved hundreds of students at different grade levels.

In Port Charlotte Middle School, Mrs. Woolley's eighth grade class scored 180% higher with *Vocabulary Cartoon* study books than did the control class that used rote memory study books.

At Cape Coral High School, English teacher Melissa Skinner's tenth grade class using *Vocabulary Cartoons* scored 105% higher, and had six times more "As" than did the control tenth grade class without the *Vocabulary Cartoon* books.

In Larry Marsh's ninth grade English classes at North Fort Myers High, fifty-five ninth grade students learned an average of 147 new words with only three hours of study. Some students learned more than one new word for every study minute.

Altogether, in double blind tests, students using *Vocabulary Cartoons* scored an average 72% higher grades than did the control students using rote memory study books.

How To Use This Book

Each page consists of four elements:

1. The **main word**. This is the word to be learned. It
is
followed by the phonetic pronunciation and a
definition.

*ACCRUE (ah KROO), v. to increase or
accumulate over time*

2. The **link word**. The link word is a simple word (or
words) which rhymes or sounds like the main word.

Link: A CREW

3. The **caption**. The caption connects the main word
and the linking word in a mnemonic rhyme.

"Pirates know how to ACCRUE A CREW."

4. The **cartoon**. The caption underscores a bizarre or
humorous cartoon which incorporates the main word
and the linking word into a visual mnemonic.

*"Pirates know how to **ACCRUE A CREW**."*

Once you make the word association between *ACCRUE* and *A CREW*, whenever you hear the word "*ACCRUE*," the linking words "*A CREW*" will come to mind to remind you of "*A CREW* being *ACCRUED*."

Use the book like flash cards, flipping through the cartoons one by one a chapter at a time. Soon you will find that the main word and its associating sound-like word link together. At about this time, the cartoon mnemonic becomes fixed in the mind's eye, and the mnemonic process is complete!

ABASHED
(ah BASHD) *adj.*
ashamed or embarrassed

Link: **CASH**

*"Tony was **ABASHED** when he
discovered he had no **CASH**."*

❑ Caught listening to her sister's conversation, Jen
was **ABASHED** and quickly put down the
receiver.

❑ Joe was not at all **ABASHED** when he opened a
valentine from Linda.

❑ My clumsiness left me **ABASHED**.

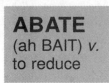

ABATE
(ah BAIT) *v.*
to reduce

Link: **BAIT**

"ABATED BAIT"

- Marta's defeat in the tennis tournament did not **ABATE** her zeal for the game.

- Tom went to a financial consultant to seek advice on **ABATING** his burdening debts.

- When the storm finally **ABATED**, we resumed our family picnic.

ABIDE
(ah BYDE) *v.*
to remain; continue; stay; endure

Link: **SIDE**

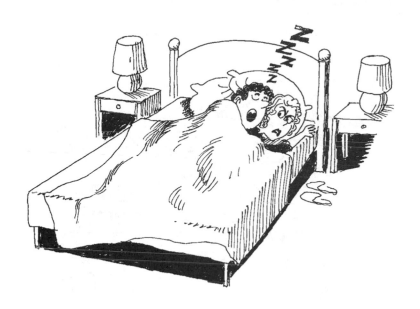

*"Ron could not **ABIDE** staying
on his **SIDE** of the bed."*

❏ The prisoner knew he had to **ABIDE** by the verdict of the jury.

❏ Josh's father always told him if he made a promise, he must **ABIDE** by it.

❏ Soldiers in battle need to have an **ABIDING** faith in their fellow soldiers.

ABLUTION

(uh BLOO shun) *n.*
a cleansing with water or other liquid, especially
as a religious ritual; the liquid used in such an act

Link: **SOLUTION**

*"The **SOLUTION** for baby's **ABLUTION**"*

- ❑ The priest performed his **ABLUTIONS** in private.

- ❑ The witch doctor used **ABLUTIONS** of clear
  water to cleanse the stricken man of his illness.

- ❑ The **ABLUTIONS** were performed in a lake near
  the temple.

ABSTRACT

(AB strakt) *adj.*
difficult to understand; abstruse;
not applied or practical

Link: **CONTRACT**

"Be wary of salesmen with
ABSTRACT CONTRACTS."

❑ Though Joshua thought his ideas were sound, we considered them **ABSTRACT**.

❑ Dad's paintings were **ABSTRACT**, we couldn't tell what they were.

❑ Christopher's directions to his house were so **ABSTRACT** that we were lost for two hours.

ACCOUNTABLE

(ah KOWNT uh bul) *adj.*
expected to answer for one's actions;
responsible, liable, answerable

Link: **COUNT THE BULLS**

*"Don, the accountant, was **ACCOUNTABLE**
for **COUNTING THE BULLS**."*

- ❏ Timothy was **ACCOUNTABLE** for counting the votes after the election.

- ❏ Laura said she was not **ACCOUNTABLE** for the problems her sister had created.

- ❏ You can't hold the cat **ACCOUNTABLE** for the mess it made because the dog chased it through the kitchen.

ACCRUE
(ah KROO) *v.*
to accumulate over time

Link: **A CREW**

*"Pirates know how to **ACCRUE A CREW**."*

- ❑ Bryan's unpaid parking tickets **ACCRUED** to the point they would have paid for his college tuition.

- ❑ By the time he was eighteen he had **ACCRUED** a good knowledge of computer skills.

- ❑ The stock dividends **ACCRUED** so rapidly that we were soon able to buy a new car.

ACME

(AK mee) *n.*
the highest point

Link: **ACNE**

*"The **ACME** of **ACNE**"*

- Because he thought the stock market had reached its **ACME**, Mr. Johnston told his stock broker to sell.

- It had been a hot morning, and the sun had not yet reached its **ACME**.

- Lisa thought the story's **ACME** was effective, but I thought the author should have told more.

ADDICT
(AD ikt) *v./n.*
to devote (oneself) habitually or
compulsively; one who is addicted

Link: **ATTIC**

*"Ed was so **ADDICTED** to cigarettes he would
sneak up in the **ATTIC** to smoke." (v.)*

❑ My mother's only regret was that she allowed
herself to become **ADDICTED** to nicotine. *(v.)*

❑ His friends worried constantly about him because
he was a drug **ADDICT**. *(n.)*

❑ Betty has become so **ADDICTED** to soap operas
she talks of nothing else. *(v.)*

ADHERENT
(ad HEER unt) *n.*
a follower of a leader; supporter

Link: **ADHERE**

*"An **ADHERENT ADHERING** to his leader"*

- ❏ The political candidate praised his **ADHERENTS** for their support.

- ❏ People who believe in a particular religion are said to be **ADHERENTS** of that faith.

- ❏ Though the divorced princess was no longer part of the royal family, she continued to claim many **ADHERENTS**.

VOCABULARY CARTOONS Review #1

Match the word with its definition.

__ 1. **abashed**	a. to accumulate over time
__ 2. **abate**	b. to remain; continue; stay; endure
__ 3. **abide**	c. a follower of a leader; supporter
__ 4. **ablution**	d. to devote (oneself) habitually
__ 5. **abstract**	e. to reduce
__ 6. **accountable**	f. the highest point
__ 7. **accrue**	g. ashamed or embarrassed
__ 8. **acme**	h. difficult to understand
__ 9. **addict**	i. a cleansing with water
__ 10. **adherent**	j. responsible

**Fill in the blanks with the most appropriate word.
The word form may need changing.**

1. Timothy was _____ for counting the votes after the election.

2. Dad's paintings were _____ , we couldn't tell what they were.

3. Caught listening to her sister's conversation, Jen was _____ and quickly put down the receiver.

4. His friends worried constantly about him because he was a drug _____ .

5. When the storm finally _____ , we resumed our family picnic.

6. The priest performed his _____ in private.

7. The political candidate praised his _____ for their support.

8. Josh's father always told him if he made a promise, he must _____ by it.

9. Because he thought the stock market had reached its _____ , Mr. Johnston told his stock broker to sell.

10. The stock dividends _____ so rapidly that we were soon able to buy a new car.

ADROIT
(uh DROIT) *adj.*
skillful; deft

Link: **DETROIT**

*"The auto workers of **DETROIT** are **ADROIT**
at manufacturing automobiles."*

❑ Many fourth graders are more **ADROIT** on the
computer than their parents.

❑ Mr. Smith **ADROITLY** removed Eric from the
class before he could cause a problem. (*adv.*)

❑ Sebastian always wins at cards because he is
so **ADROIT** at counting the cards that have been
played.

AESTHETIC
(es THET ik) *adj.*
having to do with artistic beauty

Link: **ATHLETIC**

*"Joan is both **AESTHETIC** and **ATHLETIC**."*

- ❏ Japanese rock gardens demonstrate **AESTHETIC** values typical of a Far Eastern culture.

- ❏ The artist had an uncanny sense of **AESTHETICS**; he could make a drawing of a plate of food look like a Thanksgiving feast.

- ❏ Jeannie molded the ugly lump of clay into an **AESTHETICALLY** pleasing masterpiece. (*adv.*)

AGOG

(uh GOG) *adj.*
highly excited by eagerness

Link: **EGGNOG**

*"Our dog is **AGOG** for **EGGNOG**."*

- ❏ Michelle was **AGOG** when her mom said she could spend the night at her friend's house.

- ❏ Elizabeth and Laura are always **AGOG** on Christmas morning.

- ❏ Jim sat **AGOG** when his name was announced as the winner of the Pulitzer Prize.

AMBIVALENCE
(am BIV ah lents) *n.*
indecision; experiencing
contradictory emotions

Link: **AMBULANCE**

*"**AMBIVALENCE** between two **AMBULANCES**"*

- ❑ Jim's **AMBIVALENCE** toward his boss made him regret the day he accepted the job.

- ❑ Farmer Brown was **AMBIVALENT** about whether to plant tomatoes or corn.

- ❑ Jeb's **AMBIVALENCE** about which diet to choose made him disregard the whole idea of losing weight.

AMBULATORY
(AM byu lah tor ee) *adj.*
of or for walking; capable of walking

Link: **AMBULANCE**

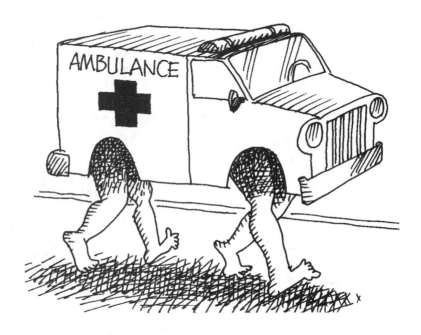

*"An **AMBULATORY AMBULANCE**"*

___

- ❑ Although Robin's foot was in a cast, she was still **AMBULATORY**.

- ❑ Most **AMBULATORY** patients do not stay overnight at the hospital.

- ❑ The ninety-eight-year-old woman was not simply **AMBULATORY**; she was spry.

ANCILLARY
(AN sih ler ee) *adj.*
helping; providing assistance; subordinate

Link: **CELERY**

*"The CELERY was ANCILLARY
to Peter's sandwich."*

❏ Christopher worked hard to earn an **ANCILLARY** income.

❏ Our chemistry workbook is **ANCILLARY** to the textbook.

❏ The queen has her **ANCILLARY** maid prepare her clothes each morning.

ANIMATED
(an eh MATE ed) *adj.*
having life; alive; filled with
activity, vigor, or spirit

Link: **ANNA MADE IT**

*"**ANNA** became **ANIMATED**
when she finally **MADE IT**."*

❏ Bill was an **ANIMATED** speaker on any subject
that interested him.

❏ Liz played the violin with intense **ANIMATION**.
(n.)

❏ Tina became highly **ANIMATED** when she heard
she was voted the "most likely to succeed."

ANIMOSITY
(an uh MAHS ih tee) *n.*
having a feeling of ill-will; bitter hostility

Link: **ANIMALS IN THE CITY**

*"The **ANIMALS IN THE CITY** showed their*
***ANIMOSITY** toward development."*

❑ The two sisters had a deep-seated **ANIMOSITY**
toward each other.

❑ Displaying **ANIMOSITY** for his neighbor, Roger
built a fence between their houses.

❑ Whenever the two rival teams encounter each
other, they show their **ANIMOSITY** by mocking
the other's mascot.

ANNALS
(ANN ulz) *n.*
descriptive record; history

Link: **HANDLES**

*"Putting **HANDLES** on the sculptured **ANNALS**"*

- ❑ The championship team of 1963 has gone down in the school's **ANNALS** as the best team of the century.

- ❑ Books having to do with the history of something are often referred to as **ANNALS**.

- ❑ The **ANNALS** of history should teach us how to avoid war.

ANNEX
(an NEKS) *v.*
to add or attach

Link: **NECKS**

*"An **ANNEXED NECK**"*

- ❏ The wedding reception was held in the **ANNEX** of the church.

- ❏ Because the school was growing so quickly, portable buildings were **ANNEXED** to the campus.

- ❏ The **ANNEX** being built adjacent to the hospital is nearly complete.

VOCABULARY CARTOONS Review #2

___ 1. **adroit**
___ 2. **aesthetic**
___ 3. **agog**
___ 4. **ambivalence**
___ 5. **ambulatory**
___ 6. **ancillary**
___ 7. **animated**
___ 8. **animosity**
___ 9. **annals**
___ 10. **annex**

a. capable of walking
b. highly excited by eagerness
c. descriptive record; history
d. filled with activity, vigor, or spirit
e. skillful; deft
f. contradictory emotions
g. to add or attach
h. having to do with artistic beauty
i. having a feeling of ill-will
j. providing assistance; subordinate

Fill in the blanks with the most appropriate word.
The word form may need changing.

1. Although Robin's foot was in a cast, she was still _____.

2. Bill was an _____ speaker on any subject that interested him.

3. Elizabeth and Laura are always _____ on Christmas morning.

4. Our chemistry workbook is _____ to the textbook.

5. Jeannie molded the ugly lump of clay into an _____ pleasing masterpiece.

6. Because the school was growing so quickly, portable buildings were _____ to the campus.

7. Many fourth graders are more _____ on the computer than their parents.

8. The _____ of history should teach us how to avoid war.

9. The two sisters had a deep-seated _____ toward each other.

10. Jim's _____ toward his boss made him regret the day he accepted the job.

APEX
(AY peks) *n.*
the highest point; peak

Link: **APE X**

*"The **APE** planted his **X** at the **APEX**."*

- ❑ Our shadows were shortest when the sun had reached its **APEX**.

- ❑ Christina marked the **APEX** before she finished the graphing problem.

- ❑ When the swing reached its **APEX**, we feared the little girl might go over the top.

APPEASE
(uh PEEZ) *v.*
to soothe; to pacify or
relieve by giving into

Link: **PEAS**

*"To **APPEASE** his parents, Johnny ate his **PEAS**."*

- ❑ To **APPEASE** his mother, Zachary always walked the dog before dinner.

- ❑ The sergeant **APPEASED** his troops by giving them an extra day of rest and relaxation.

- ❑ The trainer **APPEASES** the monkey by giving him extra bananas.

ARMAMENT

(AHR muh muhnt) *n.*
military supplies and weapons; the
process of arming for war

Link: **ARM**

*"The long **ARMS** of **ARMAMENT**"*

❑ The United States government believes its
nuclear **ARMAMENT** is a deterrent to the
possibility of a third world war.

❑ We equipped ourselves with an **ARMAMENT** no
enemy could match.

❑ Christopher is the **ARMAMENTS** officer for his
division.

ASCRIBE

(uh SKRIBE) *v.*
to attribute to a specific
cause, source, or origin

Link: **TRIBE**

*"The **TRIBE ASCRIBED** the nickname
'Long Nose' to the cavalry."*

❏ The physics professor **ASCRIBES** to the theory
that what goes up must come down.

❏ Samantha **ASCRIBED** her weight loss to a diet
of fruits and vegetables.

❏ Kurt **ASCRIBED** his gold medal to hard work
and dedication.

ASININE
(ASS uh nine) *adj.*
silly; stupid

Link: **ASS OF MINE**

*"This **ASS OF MINE** is **ASININE**."*

- ❑ My sister gave up working in a mental hospital because she could no longer deal with **ASININE** behavior.

- ❑ Adam is usually a nice guy, but sometimes he is so **ASININE** no one can stand him.

- ❑ The phone solicitor asked so many **ASININE** questions that I finally hung up.

ASSAIL
(uh SAIL) *v.*
to attack violently

Link: **SAIL**

*"A ship's **SAIL** being **ASSAILED**"*

- ❏ The debaters **ASSAILED** each other with facts, each hoping to persuade the judges to see things his way.

- ❏ While the defendant claims he did not **ASSAIL** the claimant, the claimant did have bruises to prove otherwise.

- ❏ Music **ASSAILED** our ears as we walked into the concert hall.

ATONE
(uh TONE) *v.*
to make amends

Link: **ALONE**

*"He who does not **ATONE**, ends up **ALONE**."*

- ❑ Rachel **ATONED** for skipping school by getting straight As on her next report card.

- ❑ Nothing the convicted murderer said could **ATONE** for his crime.

- ❑ After **ATONING** for his past indiscretions, the president quickly won back the support of the nation.

ATTRITION

(uh TRISH un) *n.*
a gradual reduction or
weakening; a rubbing away

Link: **FISHIN'**

"Over-FISHIN' can lead to ATTRITION."

❑ The war became a battle of **ATTRITION**, each
side wearing down the other.

❑ Because our school has so many older teachers,
the **ATTRITION** rate is high.

❑ Washed ashore, the once jagged piece of glass
had become a smoothed gem due to the
ATTRITION of the sea and sand.

AUGMENT

(awg MENT) *v.*
to make or become greater as in
size, quantity or strength

Link: **CEMENT**

*"How not to **AUGMENT** a
driveway with **CEMENT**."*

- ☐ Engineers **AUGMENTED** the engine of the fighter jet which increased its speed.

- ☐ You can **AUGMENT** the water pressure by constricting the hose nozzle.

- ☐ The president **AUGMENTED** his problems by denying his involvement in any wrong doing.

BALEFUL
(BAYL ful) *adj.*
threatening; hurtful; malignant; ominous

Link: **BAIL FALL**

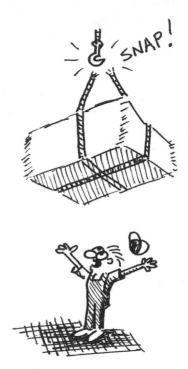

"A BALEFUL BAIL FALLING"

- ❑ The prisoner sat in **BALEFUL** silence while the judge read his jail sentence.

- ❑ Sharon cast a **BALEFUL** glance at her boyfriend when he said she had gained a lot of weight.

- ❑ The sky was **BALEFULLY** thick with clouds.

Match the word with its definition.

___ 1. **apex**   a. military supplies and weapons
___ 2. **appease**   b. silly; stupid
___ 3. **armament**   c. the highest point; peak
___ 4. **ascribe**   d. to attribute to a specific cause
___ 5. **asinine**   e. a gradual reduction
___ 6. **assail**   f. to make or become greater
___ 7. **atone**   g. to attack violently
___ 8. **attrition**   h. threatening; hurtful
___ 9. **augment**   i. to soothe
___ 10. **baleful**   j. to make amends

Fill in the blanks with the most appropriate word. The word form may need changing.

1. Music _____ our ears as we walked into the concert hall.

2. We equipped ourselves with an _____ no enemy could match.

3. The phone solicitor asked so many _____ questions that I finally hung up.

4. When the swing reached its _____ , we feared the little girl might go over the top.

5. To _____ his mother, Zachary always walked the dog before dinner.

6. Engineers _____ the engine of the fighter jet which increased its speed.

7. Sharon cast a _____ glance at her boyfriend when he said she had gained a lot of weight.

8. The physics professor _____ to the theory that what goes up must come down.

9. The war became a battle of _____ , each side wearing down the other.

10. Nothing the convicted murderer said could _____ for his crime.

BALK

(bawk) *v.*
to stop short and refuse to proceed

Link: **WALK**

*"A pirate **BALKING** at **WALKING** the plank."*

- ❑ Marcie was injured when her horse **BALKED** at the last jump in the steeplechase.

- ❑ The judge **BALKED** the hearing until order was restored in his court.

- ❑ The warden took efforts to **BALK** the escape attempt of the prisoners.

BANDY

(BAN dee) *v.*
to trade; to give back and
forth; to bat to and fro

Link: **CANDY**

*"Trick or Treaters like to **BANDY CANDY**."*

- ☐ The doctor said he wouldn't **BANDY** words; the patient needed an operation right away.

- ☐ The tennis players **BANDIED** the ball back and forth until one finally made an error and hit into the net.

- ☐ **BANDYING** arms and hands from both sides, Jenny fought her way clear and escaped from the clutches of her admiring fans.

BARRAGE

(bah RAJ) *n.*
a curtain of artillery fire; any over-
whelming attack, as of words or blows

Link: **GARAGE**

*"Our **GARAGE** was **BARRAGED**
with eggs on Halloween."*

- ❑ As soon as we stepped out of the tent we were met by a **BARRAGE** of mosquitoes.

- ❑ The attempt to attack was met by a **BARRAGE** of gunfire.

- ❑ The press shouted out a **BARRAGE** of questions as the president entered the room.

BATTERY

(BAT ur ee) *n./v.*
the unlawful beating of a person;
act of beating or pounding;

Link: **BATTERY**

"BATTERY with a BATTERY" (v.)

- Bob was arrested for **BATTERY** after a bar room brawl. *(n.)*

- After being **BATTERED** in a bar room fight, Stan was rushed to the emergency room. *(v.)*

- Bob **BATTERED** Stan with a bar stool. *(v.)*

BAUBLE
(BAW bul) *n.*
a small, inexpensive trinket

Link: **BULL**

*"A **BULL'S BAUBLE**"*

- ❑ Never one for **BAUBLES**, Diane always wore real diamonds.

- ❑ Mixed among the precious gems in Jennifer's jewelry box were costume jewelry and other **BAUBLES**.

- ❑ The child was delighted with the **BAUBLE** she received from her aunt.

BEDLAM

(BED lum) *n.*
a place or scene of noisy
uproar and confusion

Link: **BED LAMB**

"BEDLAM in the LAMB'S BED"

❑ Before the new teacher took over, there was total **BEDLAM** in the classroom.

❑ It was **BEDLAM** behind stage until the curtain went up and the play began.

❑ Following the championship soccer match, the stadium was in a state of **BEDLAM**.

BENIGHTED

(be NI tid) *adj.*
being in a state of intellectual
darkness; ignorant; unenlightened

Link: **KNIGHT**

WHAT'S THE DEAL WITH THAT GUY?

"A BENIGHTED KNIGHT"

❑ Many **BENIGHTED** people became enlightened during the Renaissance.

❑ Cameron had never read a book but was so **BENIGHTED** that he did not realize he would never be accepted into Harvard.

❑ He **BENIGHTEDLY** asked the professor how much money she would take to give him an A in her class. (*adv.*)

BEQUEST
(bi KWEST) *n.*
a legacy; something left
to someone in a will

Link: **GO WEST**

*"Joe's **BEQUEST** was to **GO WEST**."*

- ❑ If your parents leave you their house, the house is a **BEQUEST** from them to you.

- ❑ Hortensia's jewelry was a **BEQUEST** from her mother.

- ❑ **(BEQUEATH** is a verb meaning the act of leaving something in a will.) Tim's father **BEQUEATHED** his ring to his son who was pleased with the **BEQUEST**.

BEVY
(BEV ee) *n.*
a group of animals; an assemblage

Link: **HEAVY**

*"A **BEVY** of **HEAVIES**"*

- Bud's hunting dogs flushed out a **BEVY** of quail.
- A **BEVY** of groupies gathered outside to see the star after her concert.
- While hot air ballooning over the plains of Africa, one may see **BEVIES** of animals.

BLAND
(bland) *adj.*
lacking flavor or zest; dull

Link: **LAND**

*"After months at sea Columbus kissed
the **LAND**, but found it **BLAND**."*

☐ The pudding was smooth though **BLAND**.

☐ The doctor put Edgar on a **BLAND** diet to soothe
his stomach problems.

☐ Christopher's **BLAND** sense of humor was often
misunderstood.

Match the word with its definition.

__	1. **balk**	a. ignorant; unenlightened
__	2. **bandy**	b. to refuse to proceed
__	3. **barrage**	c. a small, inexpensive trinket
__	4. **battery**	d. a place or scene of noisy uproar
__	5. **bauble**	e. act of beating or pounding
__	6. **bedlam**	f. a group of animals
__	7. **benighted**	g. any overwhelming attack
__	8. **bequest**	h. to give back and forth
__	9. **bevy**	i. lacking flavor or zest; dull
__	10. **bland**	j. something left to someone

Fill in the blanks with the most appropriate word. The word form may need changing.

1. Before the new teacher took over, there was total _____ in the classroom.

2. Marcie was injured when her horse _____ at the last jump in the steeplechase.

3. The tennis players _____ the ball back and forth until one finally made an error and hit into the net.

4. A _____ of groupies gathered outside to see the star after her concert.

5. Bob was arrested for _____ after a bar room brawl.

6. Never one for _____ , Diane always wore real diamonds.

7. If your parents leave you their house, the house is a _____ from them to you.

8. The doctor put Edgar on a _____ diet to soothe his stomach problems.

9. Many _____ people became enlightened during the Renaissance.

10. The attempt to attack was met by a _____ of gunfire.

58

BOLSTER

(BOHL ster) *v./n.*
to support, as in a group; to
give a boost; a large pillow

Link: **HOLSTER**

*"Members **BOLSTERED** each other by
wearing their **HOLSTERS**." (v.)*

- ❑ The coach saw it was time to **BOLSTER** his team,
  so he gave them a pep talk. *(v.)*

- ❑ Jane knew she had to **BOLSTER** the support of
  the underclassmen if she hoped to win the
  election. *(v.)*

- ❑ Since Jackie's surgery, she has had to use a back
  BOLSTER when she sits. *(n.)*

BOMBASTIC
(bom BAS tik) *adj.*
high sounding; use of language
without much real meaning

Link: **BOMBS IN A BASKET**

*"The President's speech was so **BOMBASTIC**,
he was spitting **BOMBS IN A BASKET**."*

❏ The candidate's **BOMBASTIC** speech was hard
to understand because it made no sense.

❏ The **BOMBASTIC** article was obviously written
by a reporter who didn't do his research.

❏ Some people debate by shouting down their
opponents with **BOMBASTIC** language.

Link: **BABOON**

*"A **BOON** for **BABOONS**"*

❑ Construction of the new residential development was a **BOON** to the community.

❑ The week-long rain was a **BOON** to the farmers whose crops were withering from the drought.

❑ The decline of interest rates proved a **BOON** to the real estate market; more families could afford to buy homes.

BOORISH

(BOOR ish) *adj.*
unmannered; crude; insensitive

Link: **BOAR**

*"A **BOORISH BOAR**"*

- ❑ Bob's **BOORISH** manners at the restaurant made everyone uncomfortable.

- ❑ The **BOORISH** man pushed his way to the front of the line without any concern for others.

- ❑ Al is seldom invited to any parties because of his **BOORISH** personality.

BOOTLEG
(BOOT leg) *v.*
to smuggle; to make, sell, or
transport for sale illegally

Link: **BOOTS AND LEGS**

*"Stan was caught with **BOOTLEG
BOOTS AND LEGS**."*

- ❑ Scott was arrested when he attempted to
  BOOTLEG illegal CDs.

- ❑ During Prohibition, the **BOOTLEGGING** of alcohol
  was prevalent in the United States.

- ❑ On the streets of some cities **BOOTLEGGERS**
  sell just about anything. (*n.*)

BOOTY

(BOO tee) *n.*
loot; the spoils of war; goods or property
seized by force; a valuable prize

Link: **BOOTS**

*"Tex keeps his **BOOTY** in his **BOOTS**."*

- ❑ Some servicemen during World War II felt they were entitled to all the **BOOTY** they could capture.

- ❑ Pirates kept their **BOOTY** in chests which they sometimes buried.

- ❑ The burglars were apprehended before they could make off with the **BOOTY**.

BOVINE

(BOH vyne) *adj.*
of, relating to, or resembling an animal
such as an ox, cow or buffalo; dull

Link: **VINE**

*"A **BOVINE** on a **VINE**"*

❏ The **BOVINE** features of the man scared the
children.

❏ After examining the bones found in the field it was
determined that they were **BOVINE** remains and
not that of a human.

❏ Dr. Jones is a veterinarian who specializes in
BOVINE diseases.

BRAZEN
(BRAY zun) *adj.*
bold, shameless; impudent

Link: **RAISIN**

*"A **BRAZEN RAISIN**"*

- ❑ Robert's **BRAZEN** presumption that he would be elected class president because of his good looks proved wrong when the votes were counted.

- ❑ Tiger Woods' **BRAZEN** attempt to reach the green in two strokes paid off with a birdie.

- ❑ The senator's **BRAZEN** speech shocked the audience.

BRINK
(bringk) *n.*
edge

Link: **SINK**

*"The mice were on the **BRINK**
of falling in the **SINK**."*

❑ "My nerves are on the **BRINK**!" shouted Mom, after our rock band rehearsed in the basement all night.

❑ On the **BRINK** of disaster, Mike finally regained control of the skidding car.

❑ Grandpa Ed was on the **BRINK** of death when the paramedics arrived and saved his life.

BROUHAHA

(BROO hah hah) *n.*
an uproar; hubbub

Link: **BREW HA HA**

"The witches created a real
***BROUHAHA** while stirring their **BREW**."*

- ❑ What began as a quiet party, suddenly turned into a **BROUHAHA**.

- ❑ A **BROUHAHA** started in the government offices when a threatening e-mail was received.

- ❑ My mother warned me that if the sleep-over turned into a **BROUHAHA**, she would send all my friends home.

VOCABULARY CARTOONS Review #5

Match the word with its definition.

___ 1. **bolster**   a. property seized by force
___ 2. **bombastic**   b. bold, shameless
___ 3. **boon**   c. relating to or resembling a cow
___ 4. **boorish**   d. high sounding
___ 5. **bootleg**   e. an uproar; hubbub
___ 6. **booty**   f. to smuggle
___ 7. **bovine**   g. unmannered; crude; insensitive
___ 8. **brazen**   h. to support, as in a group
___ 9. **brink**   i. edge
__ 10. **brouhaha**   j. a timely benefit; a blessing

Fill in the blanks with the most appropriate word. The word form may need changing.

1. Scott was arrested when he attempted to _____ illegal CDs.

2. The week-long rain was a _____ to the farmers whose crops were withering from the drought.

3. Jane knew she had to _____ the support of the underclassmen if she hoped to win the election.

4. Bob's _____ manners at the restaurant made everyone uncomfortable.

5. Tiger Woods' _____ attempt to reach the green in two strokes paid off with a birdie.

6. The candidate's _____ speech was hard to understand because it made no sense.

7. On the _____ of disaster, Mike finally regained control of the skidding car.

8. Pirates kept their _____ in chests which they sometimes buried.

9. What began as a quiet party, suddenly turned into a _____.

10. The _____ features of the man scared the children.

CAMARADERIE
(kah mah RAH der ee) *n.*
comradeship; friendship

Link: **COMRADES THREE**

"CAMARADERIE amongst THREE COMRADES"

- ❏ The girls developed such a **CAMARADERIE** in college that they remained friends for life.

- ❏ People find their jobs more enjoyable if there is a sense of **CAMARADERIE** in their work place.

- ❏ Because we are both Miami Dolphins fans, we had an instant **CAMARADERIE**.

CANOPY
(KAN uh pea) *n.*
a covering

Link: **CAN OF PEAS**

*"**A CAN OF PEAS** sleeping under a **CANOPY**"*

- ☐ The hurricane blew the **CANOPY** off the garage.

- ☐ At the beach, Karen likes to sit under a **CANOPY** to protect her delicate skin from the sun.

- ☐ We sat quietly under the forest **CANOPY** and listened to all the beautiful bird calls.

CAPITULATE

(kah PICH uh layt) *v.*
to surrender under certain
conditions; to give in

Link: **CAP PITCH**

"The Foreign Legionnaires
***CAPITULATED** with a **CAP PITCH**."*

- ❑ After continuous bombing, the enemy finally
  agreed to **CAPITULATE**.

- ❑ The suspect finally **CAPITULATED** to police
  after realizing there as no escape.

- ❑ The seller studied the buyer's final offer before
  CAPITULATING and signing the contract.

CARNIVORE

(KAR ni vour) *n.*
a flesh-eating animal

Link: **DINOSAUR**

BRONTOSAURUS BURGER $1.99
MEGLADON FILET SANDWICH $2.49
TRICEROPS FRIES 99
PTERODACTYL NUGGETS . . .99

TWO BRONTOSAURUS BURGERS. HOLD THE LETTUCE AND TOMATO.

TREX

*"Some **DINOSAURS** are **CARNIVORES**."*

❑ The most famous of the **CARNIVOROUS** dinosaurs was the Tyrannosaurus Rex.

❑ Jan jokingly calls her brother a **CARNIVORE** because all he wants for dinner is meat.

❑ Alligators and crocodiles are **CARNIVORES**.

CARRION

(KAIR ee un) *n.*
dead and rotting flesh

Link: **CARRY ON**

"CARRION CARRY ON luggage"

- ❑ After mauling its prey, the lion left the **CARRION** to the hyenas.

- ❑ Days after the battle, the battlefield was littered with **CARRION** of brave soldiers.

- ❑ **CARRION** is a vulture's main source of food.

CASCADE

(kas KAYD) *n./v.*
a waterfall; to fall, pour or
rush like a waterfall

Link: **LEMONADE**

*"A **CASCADE** of **LEMONADE"** (n.)*

❑ Rachel's beautiful long hair **CASCADED** down her back. *(v.)*

❑ We decided to have our picnic near the beautiful **CASCADE**. *(n.)*

❑ When Marta hit the jackpot, coins **CASCADED** from the slot machine. *(v.)*

CATACLYSM
(KAT ah kliz um) *n.*
a violent upheaval or change

Link: **CAT CLINTON**

*"President **CLINTON'S CAT** is about
to create a **CATACLYSM**."*

❑ The **CATACLYSM** generated by World War I
had effects which lasted for generations.

❑ The sudden earthquake was **CATACLYSMIC** in
its destruction. *(adj.)*

❑ The United Nations does everything within its
power to avoid the **CATACLYSM** of a Third
World War.

CATARACT

(KAT ah rakt) *n.*
a large waterfall; a flood;
an eye abnormality

Link: **CADILLAC**

"John preferred going over the
***CATARACT** in his **CADILLAC**."*

❑ Niagara Falls is probably the most well-known
CATARACT in North America.

❑ The storm flooded the town with a **CATARACT** of
rain.

❑ The old dog developed **CATARACTS** on both his
eyes.

CAVALIER
(kav ah LEER) *adj./n.*
casual; carefree and nonchalant; arrogant
disregard; a gallant gentleman

Link: **CAVALRY**

*"Colonel Jones was **CAVALIER**
with his **CAVALRY** troops." (adj.)*

❏ We could all tell before the wedding that Phil had
   a **CAVALIER** attitude toward marriage. *(adj.)*

❏ The movie about the dashing **CAVALIERS** won
   many awards. *(n.)*

❏ Darren was so **CAVALIER** that he always kissed
   a lady's hand when first introduced. *(adj.)*

CHASTISE
(CHAS tyze) *v.*
to discipline; to criticize severely

Link: **CHEST SIZE**

*"The trainer CHASTISED John
for his puny CHEST SIZE."*

- ❑ The teacher began to **CHASTISE** her misbehaving students.

- ❑ My mother **CHASTISED** us for playing ball in the house.

- ❑ Our coach **CHASTIZED** us for losing the game.

VOCABULARY CARTOONS Review #6

Match the word with its definition.

__ 1. **camaraderie**	a. a violent upheaval or change
__ 2. **canopy**	b. carefree and nonchalant
__ 3. **capitulate**	c. comradeship; friendship
__ 4. **carnivore**	d. a flesh-eating animal
__ 5. **carrion**	e. dead and rotting flesh
__ 6. **cascade**	f. anything resembling a waterfall
__ 7. **cataclysm**	g. to discipline
__ 8. **cataract**	h. a large waterfall
__ 9. **cavalier**	i. to surrender
__ 10. **chastise**	j. a covering

Fill in the blanks with the most appropriate word. The word form may need changing.

1. We sat quietly under the forest _____ and listened to all the beautiful bird calls.

2. Alligators and crocodiles are _____.

3. After mauling its prey, the lion left the _____ to the hyenas.

4. After continuous bombing, the enemy finally agreed to _____.

5. The United Nations does everything within its power to avoid the _____ of a Third World War.

6. We could all tell before the wedding that Phil had a _____ attitude toward marriage.

7. The girls developed such a _____ in college that they remained friends for life.

8. My mother _____ us for playing ball in the house.

9. Rachel's beautiful long hair _____ down her back.

10. Niagara Falls is probably the most well-known _____ in North America.

CHOLERIC
(KAHL ur ik) *adj.*
hot-tempered; quick to anger

Link: **COLLAR**

*"Our dog became CHOLERIC
whenever we COLLARED him."*

- ❏ When my dad gets in one of his **CHOLERIC** moods, everyone stays clear.

- ❏ The neighbor's **CHOLERIC** dog is always chained to the tree.

- ❏ The bullfighter ran from the **CHOLERIC** bull.

CIRCUMSPECT
(SUR kum spekt) *adj.*
cautious; heedful of situations and
potential consequences

Link: **INSPECT**

"A CIRCUMSPECT INSPECTION"

- ❑ In his usual **CIRCUMSPECT** manner, Frank first assured himself against all losses before making an investment.

- ❑ Pat's five-year-old **CIRCUMSPECTLY** looks both ways before crossing the street. *(adv.)*

- ❑ Because the judge was **CIRCUMSPECT**, he was usually considered impartial.

CIRCUMVENT
(sur kum VENT) *v.*
to surround; enclose; bypass

Link: **CIRCLE TENT**

*"The Indians **CIRCUMVENTED** the **TENT**."*

❑ We were able to **CIRCUMVENT** the heavy traffic by taking a short-cut.

❑ The politician **CIRCUMVENTED** an argument by changing the subject.

❑ The general **CIRCUMVENTED** the enemy by distracting them with a minor campaign.

CLONE
(klohn) *n.*
an exact duplicate

Link: **CONE**

"CLONE CONES"

- ❑ The scientist **CLONED** a lab rat.
- ❑ Identical twins may be called **CLONES**.
- ❑ McDonalds restaurants are **CLONES** of each other.

COERCE
(koh URS) *v.*
to force someone by threatening or
physically overpowering him

Link: **HORSE**

WHEN I SAY GIDDY UP, I MEAN GIDDY UP!

"COERCING a HORSE"

- ❑ The burglar's confession was **COERCED** by the police.

- ❑ Elizabeth was **COERCED** by her sister to take another cookie from the jar.

- ❑ It was evident from the video tape that the hostage was **COERCED** to lie about the status of her condition.

CONFISCATE
(KON fi skayt) *v.*
to seize

Link: **CON CAKE**

*"The **CON'S CAKE** was **CONFISCATED**."*

- ❑ The teacher **CONFISCATED** Billy's gum.
- ❑ The police raided the suspect's apartment while **CONFISCATING** all his illegal drugs.
- ❑ The Internal Revenue Service threatened to **CONFISCATE** the accountant's files if he didn't pay his delinquent taxes.

CONTINUUM
(kun TIN yoo um) *n.*
a continuous whole without
clear division into parts

Link: **CONTINUE**

*"A beam of light is a **CONTINUUM**
which **CONTINUES** from its source."*

❑ A spectrum of light is a **CONTINUUM** in which
each color blends with its neighbors.

❑ At the carnival, a **CONTINUUM** of weaving
dances moved in a seemingly endless chain.

❑ Albert Einstein believed that space and time are
not distinct dimensions, but a **CONTINUUM**,
which he called the Theory of Relativity.

CONUNDRUM
(kuh NUN drum) *n.*
a dilemma; any problem or puzzle

Link: **NUN'S DRUM**

*"The **NUN'S DRUMS** created a **CONUNDRUM**."*

- In most mystery novels, the **CONUNDRUM** is solved by the end.

- Justin's **CONUNDRUM** after high school was whether he should go find a job or go to college first.

- During the long drive, Jean invented entertaining **CONUNDRUMS** to help keep Jeff awake.

COPIOUS
(KOH pee us) *adj.*
abundant; plentiful

Link: **CUP**

*"A **COPIOUS CUP** of coffee"*

- ❑ Farmer Brown was overjoyed with his **COPIOUS** crop of tomatoes.

- ❑ David gave **COPIOUS** reasons why he should be allowed to stay home from school.

- ❑ Professor Lang always gave long lectures and expected his students to take **COPIOUS** notes in history class.

CORPULENT
(KOR pew lent) *n.*
fat; obese

Link: **CORPORAL**

*"A **CORPULENT CORPORAL**"*

❑ England's King Henry VIII was known for his **CORPULENT** build.

❑ Some football players look **CORPULENT** but are actually very muscular.

❑ **CORPULENT** is a euphemism for fat.

Match the word with its definition.

__	1. **choleric**	a.	abundant; plentiful
__	2. **circumspect**	b.	a dilemma or problem
__	3. **circumvent**	c.	hot-tempered; quick to anger
__	4. **clone**	d.	an exact duplicate
__	5. **coerce**	e.	to surround; enclose; bypass
__	6. **confiscate**	f.	a continuous whole
__	7. **continuum**	g.	fat; obese
__	8. **conundrum**	h.	to seize
__	9. **copious**	i.	to force someone by threatening
__	10. **corpulent**	j.	cautious

**Fill in the blanks with the most appropriate word.
The word form may need changing.**

1. The burglar's confession was _____ by the police.

2. The teacher _____ Billy's gum.

3. In most mystery novels, the _____ is solved by the end.

4. In his usual _____ manner, Frank first assured himself against all losses before making an investment.

5. The scientist _____ a lab rat.

6. We were able to _____ the heavy traffic by taking a short-cut.

7. Some football players look _____ but are actually very muscular.

8. When my dad gets in one of his _____ moods, everyone stays clear.

9. Farmer Brown was overjoyed with his _____ crop of tomatoes.

10. Albert Einstein believed that space and time are not distinct dimensions, but a _____ , which he called the Theory of Relativity.

COURIER

(KUR ee ur) *n.*
a messenger

Link: **CARRY HER**

*"The **CARRY HER COURIER** Service"*

- ❑ The **COURIER** delivered an important letter from the general.

- ❑ Frederick works as a **COURIER** for United Parcel Service.

- ❑ The spy acted as a **COURIER**, carrying secret information between the United States and Europe.

COVERT
(KOH vert) *adj.*
secret; hidden; concealed

Link: **COVER**

*"Secret agents **COVERTLY**
COVER their true identities."* *(adv.)*

□ Sam carried out **COVERT** missions for the CIA in China during the Korean War.

□ Spies usually operate **COVERTLY**. *(adv.)*

□ OVERT is the opposite of **COVERT**. OVERT means open or unconcealed.

CRONY
(KROH nee) *n.*
a close friend or companion

Link: **BOLOGNA**

*"A **BOLOGNA** and his **CRONY**"*

- ❏ Jim and his **CRONIES** go to the football games on Friday nights.

- ❏ John Dillinger and his **CRONIES** robbed the First National Bank.

- ❏ Edward is honored to be considered one of his boss's **CRONIES**.

CRUX

(KRUKS) *n.*
main point; the heart of the matter

Link: **DUCKS**

*"The **DUCKS** were the **CRUX** of the traffic jam."*

- ❏ After Harry rambled on for hours, it was difficult to understand the **CRUX** of his speech.

- ❏ The mechanic thought the **CRUX** of the car's problem was a bad water pump.

- ❏ The **CRUX** of the plot happened just when the suspense was unbearable.

CRYPTIC
(KRIP tik) *adj.*
having an ambiguous or
hidden meaning

Link: **LIPSTICK**

*"A **CRYPTIC** note in **LIPSTICK**"*

- ❑ Jim's messages were so **CRYPTIC**; I was baffled by their meaning.

- ❑ Breaking Germany's **CRYPTIC** codes during World War II helped the Allies win the war.

- ❑ While exploring the cave, we stumbled across a **CRYPTIC** message written on the wall.

CUPIDITY

(kyoo PID ih tee) *n.*

excessive greed, especially for money

Link: **CUPID**

"CUPID'S CUPIDITY"

❏ The thief's **CUPIDITY** was exceeded only by his ignorance.

❏ Bob's obsessive **CUPIDITY** alienated him from his family and friends, because all he could think about is making money.

❏ The **CUPIDITY** of the Roman upper-class led to the demise of the Roman Empire.

CURB

(kurb) *v.*
to control or check

Link: **HERB**

*"**HERB** could not **CURB** his love of flying."*

- ❏ Weight Watchers' mission is to help corpulent people **CURB** their appetites.

- ❏ She wore a nicotine patch to try to **CURB** her addiction to smoking.

- ❏ By making them raise their hands, the new teacher **CURBED** her students' tendency to shout out the answers.

CURSORY

(KUR suh ree) *adj.*
rapid and superficial; performed with
haste and scant attention to detail

Link: **CURSE**

*"A **CURSORY** glance by the prince told
him Cinderella's foot had been **CURSED**."*

- ❑ Dad's **CURSORY** effort to repair the roof made it leak even more.

- ❑ The general berated the private for his **CURSORY** attempt to clean his locker.

- ❑ The general contractor was so **CURSORY** in the construction of our home that he forgot to lay the plumbing lines.

DEFUNCT
(dee FUNGKT) *adj.*
dead or inactive; having
ceased to exist

Link: **JUNK**

*"Chinese **JUNKS** are now **DEFUNCT**."*

❑ The invention of the automobile made riding a
horse and carriage a **DEFUNCT** mode of
transportation.

❑ Although Shakespeare has been dead for
centuries, his plays will never be **DEFUNCT**.

❑ In *Moby Dick*, Ishmael tells the story of a
DEFUNCT whaling ship, the *Pequod*.

DEMISE
(dih MIZE) *n.*
death; the end

Link: **EYES**

*"The **EYES** told of Dracula's **DEMISE**."*

- ❑ Chuck was devastated by the **DEMISE** of his pet turtle.

- ❑ General George Custer met his **DEMISE** at Little Big Horn.

- ❑ Joe's broken leg led to the **DEMISE** of his football career.

Match the word with its definition.

___	1. **courier**	a. the main point
___	2. **covert**	b. excessive greed
___	3. **crony**	c. having ceased to exist
___	4. **crux**	d. secret; hidden; concealed
___	5. **cryptic**	e. death; the end
___	6. **cupidity**	f. a close friend
___	7. **curb**	g. performed with haste
___	8. **cursory**	h. a messenger
___	9. **defunct**	i. to control or check
___	10. **demise**	j. having a hidden meaning

Fill in the blanks with the most appropriate word.
The word form may need changing.

1. She wore a nicotine patch to try to _____ her addiction to smoking.

2. Bob's obsessive _____ alienated him from his family and friends, because all he could think about is making money.

3. Dad's _____ effort to repair the roof made it leak even more.

4. After Harry rambled on for hours, it was difficult to understand the _____ of his speech.

5. Chuck was devastated by the _____ of his pet turtle.

6. Sam carried out _____ missions for the CIA in China during the Korean War.

7. John Dillinger and his _____ robbed the First National Bank.

8. The invention of the automobile made riding a horse and carriage a _____ mode of transportation.

9. The _____ delivered an important letter from the general.

10. Breaking Germany's _____ codes during World War II helped the Allies win the war.

DEPLOY
(dih PLOY) *v.*
to arrange strategically

Link: **TOY**

*"David **DEPLOYED** his **TOYS** to attack his sister."*

- The general's intelligent **DEPLOYMENT** of his troops along the eastern front won the battle. (*n.*)

- The admiral **DEPLOYED** his ships at the entrance to the harbor.

- By **DEPLOYING** all his resources, Phil was able to buy the car.

DEPRAVITY
(dih PRAV ih tee) *n.*
extreme wickedness

Link: **CAVITY**

*"Dr. Hook has a **DEPRAVITY** for **CAVATIES**."*

- ❏ Ed's mother attributed his **DEPRAVITY** to violent movies and video games.

- ❏ Muhammad Ali was famous in the ring for his **DEPRAVITY** toward opposing boxers.

- ❏ The principal could not believe Jason was capable of such **DEPRAVED** activities. *(adj.)*

DEPRECATE
(DEP ri kayt) *v.*
to express disapproval of

Link: **DEBRA'S CAKE**

*"No one dared **DEPRECATE DEBRA'S CAKE**."*

- ❏ Josh's parents **DEPRECATED** his study habits of always waiting to the last minute.

- ❏ The teacher was **DEPRECATORY** when she realized no one had completed the assignment. *(adj.)*

- ❏ Jerry Seinfeld and many other comics are famous for self-**DEPRECATING** humor. *(adj.)*

DESPOT
(DES puht) *n.*
an absolute ruler

Link: **THIS POT**

"THIS POT is the DESPOT."

- ❑ The **DESPOT** declared his birthday a national holiday.

- ❑ My big brother thinks he is the **DESPOT** of the family; he is always bossing everyone around.

- ❑ When mom gives us our chores, she rules us like a **DESPOT**.

DETER

(dih TUR) *v.*
to discourage; to keep someone
from doing something

Link: **WEATHER**

*"**WEATHER** never **DETERRED**
Jody from playing golf."*

- ❑ Nothing could **DETER** John from his ambition to be a doctor.

- ❑ Rachel didn't let her handicap **DETER** her from competing in the triathlon.

- ❑ Bryan's broken leg **DETERRED** him from playing softball.

DEVOID
(dih VOID) *adj.*
entirely without; lacking

Link: **AVOID**

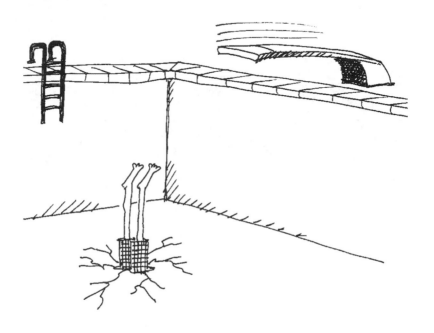

*"**AVOID** diving into a pool **DEVOID** of water."*

- ❏ It was apparent that Bill was **DEVOID** of table manners as we watched him eat his entire meal with his fingers.

- ❏ The small deserted island was **DEVOID** of drinking water.

- ❏ Our football team is totally **DEVOID** of an offense; we haven't scored a touchdown in the last four games.

DIATRIBE
(DYE uh tryb) *n.*
a bitter verbal attack

Link: **TRIBE**

*"Sitting Bull retaliated with a **DIATRIBE**
after his **TRIBE** was pied in the face."*

❑ Coach Johnson's **DIATRIBE** was futile because
the referee refused to reverse his decision.

❑ The prosecuting attorney began his opening
statement with a **DIATRIBE** directed toward the
defendant.

❑ After being struck by a water balloon, the old man
retaliated with a lengthy **DIATRIBE** which scared
away the deviant kids.

DIFFIDENT
(DIF ih dent) *adj.*
lacking self-confidence; timid

Link: **DIFFERENT**

*"Is Lord Wellington **DIFFIDENT** about
swimming or is he **DIFFERENT**?"*

- ❏ The **DIFFIDENT** boy always sat alone in the cafeteria.

- ❏ In order to assuage her **DIFFIDENCE**, Beth was persuaded to enroll in drama class. *(n.)*

- ❏ The **DIFFIDENT** kitten was stuck up in the tree for hours.

DIMINUTION
(dih muh NYOO shun) *n.*
the act or process of diminishing; reduction

Link: **AMMUNITION**

*"A **DIMINUTION** of **AMMUNITION**"*

- ❑ The crew of the crippled research submarine were concerned with the **DIMINUTION** of their air supply.

- ❑ There was an obvious **DIMINUTION** of the temperature as the sun began to set.

- ❑ Due to the higher cost of living, Drew noticed a **DIMINUTION** of his checking account.

DIRE

(DYE ur) *adj.*
disastrous; desperate

Link: **FIRE**

*"A **DIRE FIRE**"*

- ❑ The hurricane struck the Florida Keys with **DIRE** results; all the buildings were flattened.

- ❑ After the girls' wallets were stolen on vacation, they were in **DIRE** straits; they had no money, no shelter, and not even a quarter to call home.

- ❑ Jeff's **DIRE** predictions about a stock market crash unfortunately came true, and now everyone in his family is broke.

VOCABULARY CARTOONS Review #9

___ 1. **deploy**   a. extreme wickedness
___ 2. **depravity**   b. a bitter verbal attack
___ 3. **deprecate**   c. to discourage
___ 4. **despot**   d. entirely without; lacking
___ 5. **deter**   e. to express disapproval of
___ 6. **devoid**   f. to arrange strategically
___ 7. **diatribe**   g. the act or process of diminishing
___ 8. **diffident**   h. disastrous; desperate
___ 9. **diminution** i. lacking self-confidence; timid
___ 10. **dire**   j. an absolute ruler

1. Nothing could _____ John from his ambition to be a doctor.

2. The small deserted island was _____ of drinking water.

3. Josh's parents _____ his study habits of always waiting to the last minute.

4. The admiral _____ his ships at the entrance to the harbor.

5. Ed's mother attributed his _____ to violent movies and video games.

6. The prosecuting attorney began his opening statement with a _____ directed toward the defendant.

7. The hurricane struck the Florida Keys with _____ results; all the buildings were flattened.

8. The _____ declared his birthday a national holiday.

9. The crew of the crippled research submarine were concerned with the _____ of their air supply.

10. The _____ boy always sat alone in the cafeteria.

DISCONCERT
(dis cun SURT) *v.*
to disturb the composure of; upset; to
frustrate (as a plan) by throwing into disorder

Link: **THIS CONCERT**

*"**THIS CONCERT** is
DISCONCERTING to my father."*

❑ Some students find it very **DISCONCERTING** to
listen to music while studying.

❑ At times a baby may be unaffected by loud
noises while at others it may be
DISCONCERTED by a quiet sound.

❑ I don't mean to **DISCONCERT** your plans, but I
can't attend your party on Saturday.

DISHEVEL

(dih SHEV ul) *v.*
to make untidy; to disarrange
the hair or clothing of

Link: **SHOVEL**

*"Tommy DISHEVELED his
aunt with his SHOVEL."*

- ❑ Andrea's hair became **DISHEVELED** in the strong breeze.

- ❑ After the hurricane, our yard was **DISHEVELED** with broken branches and debris.

- ❑ From the looks of Bryan's **DISHEVELED** desk, one would think he is a disorganized person.

DIURNAL

(dye UR nul) *adj.*
occurring every day; occurring during the daytime

Link: **DAY TURTLE**

*"A **DIURNAL TURTLE**"*

- ❏ Brad enjoys his **DIURNAL** cup of coffee while he reads the newspaper.

- ❏ Sunrise is a **DIURNAL** occurrence.

- ❏ **DIURNAL** is the opposite of nocturnal, which means occurring during the night.

DIVERSE
(dih VURS) *adj.*
different; varied

Link: **DIVERS**

"DIVERSE sky DIVERS"

- ❑ Humphrey had a **DIVERSE** collection of classic automobiles.

- ❑ The California Gold Rush attracted people of **DIVERSE** backgrounds: farmers, bankers, and tradesmen made the journey to the gold fields.

- ❑ Randy had a **DIVERSE** education with degrees in medicine, law, and business.

DOFF
(dof) *v.*
to take off; to remove

Link: **OFF**

"To DOFF is to take OFF."

❑ A gentleman should always **DOFF** his hat to a lady.

❑ The football player ran to the sideline, **DOFFED** his helmet and downed a huge cup of water.

❑ The nurse instructed me to **DOFF** my clothes and don a hospital robe.

DOGMATIC

(dawg MAT ik) *adj.*
characterized by an authoritative, often
arrogant, assertion of opinions or beliefs

Link: **DOG**

*"A **DOGMATIC DOG** trainer"*

- Grandpa was always **DOGMATIC** about his views on politics.

- The tyrant was a **DOGMATICAL** ruler who would not permit anyone to disagree with him.

- The opinions or ideas **DOGMATICALLY** asserted by a **DOGMATIC** person are known as **DOGMA**. *(adv./adj./n.)*

DOLEFUL
(DOHL ful) *adj.*
sorrowful; melancholy

Link: **BOWL FULL**

BILLY, YOU HAVE TO EAT YOUR SPLIT PEA SOUP BEFORE YOU CAN GO OUT TO PLAY.

*"Billy was **DOLEFUL** because he had to eat a **BOWL FULL** of split pea soup."*

❑ The **DOLEFUL** expression on the dog's face suggested he thought he had been deserted by his owner.

❑ A **DOLEFUL** procession of mourners followed the hearse to the cemetery.

❑ When the doctor arrived to see her ailing husband, Jim's wife **DOLEFULLY** opened the door to let him in. *(adv.)*

Link: **VOLT**

*"A **DOLT** gets the **VOLTS**"*

- ❑ The frustrated teacher said he had a class full of **DOLTS**.

- ❑ Only a **DOLT** would put his shoes on backward.

- ❑ Dad always said, "Don't be a **DOLT** and stay in school."

DON
(don) *v.*
to put on

Link: **ON**

*"To **DON** is to put **ON**."*

- ❏ Bryan **DONNED** his scuba gear and rolled off the boat into the ocean.

- ❏ Ed took a deep breath, **DONNED** his parachute, and jumped out of the airplane.

- ❏ As the storm intensified, Bill went below deck to **DON** his foul weather gear.

DOUR
(dowr) *adj.*
severe; gloomy; stern

Link: **FLOWER**

*"A **DOUR FLOWER**"*

- ❑ The garbage collector was a **DOUR** older man who never had a kind word for anyone.

- ❑ When the legionnaire begged the Arab for water, the Arab **DOURLY** replied he barely had enough for his camel. *(adv.)*

- ❑ The barren **DOURNESS** of the infertile land on their farm made it almost impossible for Tim's family to make a living as farmers. *(n.)*

Match the word with its definition.

__ 1.	**disconcert**	a. sorrowful; melancholy
__ 2.	**dishevel**	b. to disturb the composure of
__ 3.	**diurnal**	c. to remove
__ 4.	**diverse**	d. an arrogant assertion of opinions
__ 5.	**doff**	e. to put on
__ 6.	**dogmatic**	f. different; varied
__ 7.	**doleful**	g. to make untidy
__ 8.	**dolt**	h. severe; gloomy; stern
__ 9.	**don**	i. occurring during the daytime
__10.	**dour**	j. a stupid person

Fill in the blanks with the most appropriate word. The word form may need changing.

1. The frustrated teacher said he had a class full of _____.

2. Brad enjoys his _____ cup of coffee while he reads the newspaper.

3. A _____ procession of mourners followed the hearse to the cemetery.

4. Andrea's hair became _____ in the strong breeze.

5. Grandpa was always _____ about his views on politics.

6. Some students find it very _____ to listen to music while studying.

7. Bryan _____ his scuba gear and rolled off the boat into the ocean.

8. Humphrey had a _____ collection of classic automobiles.

9. The garbage collector was a _____ older man who never had a kind word for anyone.

10. The football player ran to the sideline, _____ his helmet and downed a huge cup of water.

DWELL

(dwel) *v.*
to remain for a time; to reside; to focus
attention on; to speak or write about at length

Link: **HILL**

*"Ants **DWELL** in a **HILL**."*

❑ Our coach told the team not to **DWELL** on losing
one game and start thinking about winning the
next.

❑ The newspaper article **DWELLS** on the need for
better schools.

❑ Don't **DWELL** on the negative; think of the
positive.

EBULLIENCE
(ih BULL yents) *n.*
lots of enthusiasm; bubbling with

Link: **BULL DANCE**

"EBULLIENCE at the BULL DANCE"

- ❑ Chris's **EBULLIENT** personality won her many friends. *(adj.)*

- ❑ Joan's **EBULLIENCE** for her work is obvious in her time and effort.

- ❑ The bride's **EBULLIENCE** was evident in way she interacted with her guests.

EDIFICATION
(ed ih fih KAY shun) *n.*
enlighten; instruct

Link: **ED ON VACATION**

*"**ED** is getting some **EDIFICATION**
while he is **ON VACATION**."*

❑ Many parents send their children to Sunday
School for moral **EDIFICATION**.

❑ Etiquette is an important part of one's social
EDIFICATION.

❑ We would have been lost at the art show had not
programs been provided for our **EDIFICATION**.

EGG

(eg) *v.*
to encourage or incite to action

Link: **EGG**

*"Humpty was **EGGED** to jump."*

- ❑ The bully **EGGED** the little boy to fight until he cried.

- ❑ My friends **EGGED** me to try out for the tennis team.

- ❑ Without the crowd **EGGING** me on, I don't think I could have finished running the marathon.

ELITE
(eh LEET) *n.*
the best or most skilled
members of a group

Link: **FEET**

*"The **ELITE** wine makers have big **FEET**."*

- ❑ Members of the school's academic teams are among the educational **ELITE**.

- ❑ The city was defended by an **ELITE** corps of soldiers. *(adj.)*

- ❑ An **ELITIST** is a snob; to be **ELITIST** is to be snobby.

ELOCUTION

(el oh KYOO shun) *n.*
the art of public speaking

Link: **EXECUTION**

*"**ELOCUTION** is a good way to
postpone an **EXECUTION**."*

- ☐ Classes in **ELOCUTION** are helpful to those who seek a career in politics.

- ☐ The Greek orator Demosthenes had a speech impediment, but he taught himself proper **ELOCUTION** by reciting poetry.

- ☐ Mark Twain was known for his **ELOCUTION** as well as his stories.

ELOQUENT

(EL oh kwent) *adj.*
extremely expressive in speech,
writing, or movement

Link: **ELEPHANT**

EVERYONE PARTISON TO THIS MAGNIFICENT CRUSADE AGAINST IVORY POACHERS MUST MAKE A PRODIGOUS EFFORT IN SUPPORT OF OUR NOBLE CAUSE.

*"An **ELOQUENT ELEPHANT**"*

❏ Stan gave a moving, **ELOQUENT** speech.

❏ Shakespeare's plays are very **ELOQUENTLY**
written. *(adv.)*

❏ As the queen approached, the knight responded
with an **ELOQUENT** bow.

ELUCIDATE
(ih LOO si dayt) *v.*
to make clear and explain fully

Link: **LUCY DATE**

*"**LUCY**, Gary's blind **DATE**,*
***ELUCIDATED** her intentions."*

- ❏ Greg **ELUCIDATED** his description of the assailant to the officer.

- ❏ Doctors should always **ELUCIDATE** the medical jargon they use with their patients.

- ❏ Brian Williams had a gift for **ELUCIDATING** news to his national TV audience.

EMBROIL
(im BROYL) *v.*
to involve in argument or hostile
action; to throw in disorder

Link: **BOIL**

*"The lobster preferred **EMBROILING** to **BOILING**."*

❑ Most of the civilized world was **EMBROILED** in
   conflict during World War II.

❑ The attorneys were **EMBROILED** in caustic
   argument.

❑ An **EMBROILING** situation arose when the rock
   concert was cancelled. *(adj.)*

EMINENT

(EM ih nent) *adj.*
standing out, renowned;
distinguished; prominent

Link: **EMMA'S TENT**

*"EMMA'S TENT was the most
EMINENT of the girl scouts tents."*

❑ Michael Jordan is considered one of the most
EMINENT basketball players of the 20th century.

❑ The most **EMINENT** feature of the hammerhead
shark is its hammer-shaped head.

❑ The audience fell silent when the **EMINENT**
singer walked on stage.

Match the word with its definition.

___ 1. **dwell**   a. to encourage
___ 2. **ebullience**   b. to involve in argument
___ 3. **edification**   c. to remain for a time; to reside
___ 4. **egg**   d. standing out, renowned
___ 5. **elite**   e. to make clear and explain fully
___ 6. **elocution**   f. enlighten; instruct
___ 7. **eloquent**   g. the best members of a group
___ 8. **elucidate**   h. bubbling with excitement
___ 9. **embroil**   i. the art of public speaking
___ 10. **eminent**   j. extremely expressive in speech

Fill in the blanks with the most appropriate word. The word form may need changing.

1. Classes in _____ are helpful to those who seek a career in politics.

2. Members of the school's academic teams are among the educational _____.

3. Our coach told the team not to _____ on losing one game and start thinking about winning the next.

4. Stan gave a moving, _____ speech.

5. Joan's _____ for her work is obvious in her time and effort.

6. The most _____ feature of the hammerhead shark is its hammer-shaped head.

7. Many parents send their children to Sunday School for moral _____.

8. Greg _____ his description of the assailant to the officer.

9. Without the crowd _____ me on, I don't think I could have finished running the marathon.

10. Most of the civilized world was _____ in conflict during World War II.

135

EMPHATIC
(em FAT ik) *adj.*
forcibly expressive

Link: **FAT TICK**

*"Rex became **EMPHATIC** when he saw a **FAT TICK** on his back."*

❏ The scientist was **EMPHATIC** that no flammable materials be brought to the test site.

❏ The crowd's **EMPHATIC** reaction of their team winning the game was a sight to see.

❏ The sign **EMPHATICALLY** warned visitors to keep their hands out of the cage. *(adv.)*

ENHANCE
(en HANS) *v.*
to improve; to intensify

Link: **DANCE**

"The band thought new speakers would
***ENHANCE** the **DANCE** music."*

❑ Sheila believed applying a lot of makeup would
ENHANCE her looks, when in reality it made her
look like a clown.

❑ Bob **ENHANCED** his race car's performance by
installing a more powerful engine.

❑ Since **ENHANCING** my computer's modem, I am
able to do research more quickly.

ENMITY

(EN mi tee) *n.*
hostility; deep-seated hatred

Link: **IN MY TEA**

*"Sir Howard, I have great **ENMITY** for your dog's tongue **IN MY TEA**."*

- ❏ The **ENMITY** between the teams was apparent to the spectators.

- ❏ When she saw his new girlfriend, it was not easy to disguise her **ENMITY**.

- ❏ The **ENMITY** between the feuding families is very obvious in the book.

ESCAPADE
(ES kah payd) *n.*
an adventurous unconventional act

Link: **ICE CAPADES**

*"An **ESCAPADE** at the **ICE CAPADES**"*

- ❑ Mary's **ESCAPADE** was harmless, but it caused her parents some concern.

- ❑ Joe and Alan's **ESCAPADE** at the beach during spring break is one they will never forget.

- ❑ Hiking in the Rockies was our most recent family **ESCAPADE**.

ESCHEW
(es CHOO) *v.*
to avoid or shun

Link: **AH CHEW**

*"It is a good policy to **ESCHEW** all **AH CHEWS**!"*

- ❑ We were advised to **ESCHEW** riding the subway at night.

- ❑ The doctor told Danny to **ESCHEW** the sun's dangerous rays by applying sunscreen whenever he went outside.

- ❑ Sally **ESCHEWS** anyone who uses bad language.

ESPOUSE
(eh SPOWZ) *v.*
to adopt; to support

Link: **SPOUSE**

*"Harold's **SPOUSE ESPOUSED** a large family."*

- ❏ I **ESPOUSE** the idea that we eat dessert before dinner.

- ❏ The candidate for governor **ESPOUSED** a one-cent sales tax to build a new stadium.

- ❏ Because Barbara was always ready to **ESPOUSE** students' privileges, she was elected senior class president.

ESTRANGE

(eh STRAINJ) *v.*
to alienate; to treat as a stranger; to turn an affectionate attitude into an indifferent or unfriendly one

Link: **STRANGE**

*"Nancy became **ESTRANGED** from her husband because he was so **STRANGE**."*

❏ Lawrence feared his candid views of the company would **ESTRANGE** him from his coworkers.

❏ Hardly recognizing anyone, Ed felt **ESTRANGED** from his old high school classmates during his 25th reunion.

❏ The governor stated that capital punishment does not deter crime, and in so doing **ESTRANGED** himself from many of his erstwhile supporters.

ETHEREAL
(ih THEER ee ul) *adj.*
very light; airy; delicate; heavenly

Link: **CEREAL**

"ETHEREAL CEREAL"

- ❑ An **ETHEREAL** mist covered the hill in the morning.

- ❑ The **ETHEREAL** scent of freshly baked apple pie permeated the kitchen.

- ❑ Elizabeth had the singing voice of an **ETHEREAL** angel.

EVINCE
(ih VINCE) *v.*
to show or demonstrate clearly

Link: **EVENTS**

*"EVENTS soon would EVINCE
Tom's short-sightedness."*

❏ The prince wished to **EVINCE** his love for the fair maiden.

❏ The new billboard **EVINCED** our sales message.

❏ Ed spent hours **EVINCING** the perfect technique of throwing the shot putt.

EXALT
(ig ZAWLT) *v.*
to raise high; glorify

Link: **SALT**

*"Everyone **EXALTED** the **SALT** as
king of the condiments."*

❑ The fireman was **EXALTED** by the press for
saving the child from a burning building.

❑ Elizabeth felt **EXALTED** when she scored 1600
on her SAT.

❑ Our society tends to **EXALT** actors and sport
stars rather than teachers and professors.

Match the word with its definition.

__	1. **emphatic**	a. to alienate
__	2. **enhance**	b. an adventurous act
__	3. **enmity**	c. to adopt; to support
__	4. **escapade**	d. hostility; deep-seated hatred
__	5. **eschew**	e. to show or demonstrate clearly
__	6. **espouse**	f. to raise high; glorify
__	7. **estrange**	g. to avoid or shun
__	8. **ethereal**	h. very light; airy; delicate
__	9. **evince**	i. forcibly expressive
__	10. **exalt**	j. to improve; to intensify

Fill in the blanks with the most appropriate word. The word form may need changing.

1. An _____ mist covered the hill in the morning.

2. The _____ between the teams was apparent to the spectators.

3. We were advised to _____ riding the subway at night.

4. Sheila believed applying a lot of makeup would _____ her looks; when in reality it made her look like a clown.

5. Hiking in the Rockies was our most recent family _____.

6. Hardly recognizing anyone, Ed felt _____ from his old high school classmates during his 25th reunion.

7. The scientist was _____ that no flammable materials be brought to the test site.

8. The fireman was _____ by the press for saving the child from a burning building.

9. The candidate for governor _____ a one-cent sales tax to build a new stadium.

10. The prince wished to _____ his love for the fair maiden.

EXEMPLAR
(ig ZEM pler) *n.*
a model or original

Link: **EXAMPLE**

*"An **EXAMPLE** of an **EXEMPLARY** dog." (adj.)*

❑ Charlie has always been an **EXEMPLARY** student. *(adj.)*

❑ Notre Dame, in Paris, is an **EXAMPLAR** of a historic Roman Catholic Marian cathedral.

❑ Shakespeare's poetic form is an **EXEMPLAR** of iambic pentameter.

EXODUS
(EK suh dus) *n.*
a mass departure

Link: **EXIT BUS**

*"A **BUS EXODUS** from the rear **EXIT**"*

- ❏ There was an immediate **EXODUS** of people from the theater when someone yelled, "Fire!"

- ❏ After the hurricane evacuation was announced, there was mass **EXODUS** of people from the town.

- ❏ The forest fire created an **EXODUS** of animals.

EXONERATE
(ig ZON er ate) *v.*
to free from accusation or blame; to
free from a responsibility or task

Link: **HIS HONOR WAS LATE**

*"**HIS HONOR WAS** too **LATE** to
EXONERATE the innocent prisoner."*

- ❑ When he was released from jail, he finally felt **EXONERATED** of his crime.

- ❑ The general wanted to **EXONERATE** the captain of his war crimes.

- ❑ The man was **EXONERATED** by a jury of his peers even though public opinion was not on his side.

EXPATRIATE

(eks PAY tree ayt) *v./n.*

to exile, banish; leave one's country (either by force or by desire); one who has taken up residence in a foreign country

Link: **PATRIOT**

"EXPATRIATING a PATRIOT" *(v.)*

❑ Fidel Castro **EXPATRIATED** many of Cuba's former **PATRIOTS** who no longer agreed with him. *(v.)*

❑ Some American communists **EXPATRIATED** to the Soviet Union during the Cold War. *(v.)*

❑ Ernest Hemingway was an American **EXPATRIATE** who lived in Cuba. *(n.)*

EXTRUDE
(ik STROOD) *v.*
to force out, as through a small opening

Link: **INTRUDE**

*"An **INTRUDER** gets **EXTRUDED**"*

- ❑ Toothpaste **EXTRUDES** from the tube when you squeeze it.

- ❑ Black oil **EXTRUDED** from the engine block.

- ❑ The molten rock **EXTRUDED** from the fissure in the side of the mountain.

FETTER

(FET ur) *v./n.*
to restrain; to hamper; a shackle

Link: **FEATHER**

"A FETTERED FEATHER" (v.)

- ❑ The prisoners were **FETTERED** by shackles around their ankles. (*v.*)

- ❑ The cowboy **FETTERED** his horse so it would still be there when he wanted to go home. (*v.*)

- ❑ The prisoner's **FETTER** was attached to his ankles, preventing him from running. (*n.*)

FIASCO
(fee AS koh) *n.*
a complete or humiliating failure

Link: **TABASCO**

*"A **TABASCO FIASCO**"*

- ❑ The children's plan to release all the animals at the Humane Society was an utter **FIASCO**.

- ❑ Our government has been involved in numerous **FIASCOES** which will go down in history.

- ❑ Teresa ordered $300 worth of Girl Scout cookies and her parents had to pay for the **FIASCO**.

FORBEARANCE

(for BEAR unts) *n.*
a refraining from the enforcement
of something; patience

Link: **FOUR PARENTS**

"FOUR PARENTS exhibiting FORBEARANCE"

- ❏ Sitting in traffic on the highway requires great **FORBEARANCE**.

- ❏ The hunter showed great **FORBEARANCE** by sitting in the tree stand all day long.

- ❏ Social workers must possess **FORBEARANCE** to deal with their difficult clients.

FOREBODE
(for BODE) *v.*
to predict or foretell

Link: **FOUR BONES**

"The gypsy FOREBODED
FOUR BONES in Rex's future."

- ❑ In ancient Greece it was believed that a sage could **FOREBODE** the future.

- ❑ A **FOREBODING** rain began working its way toward us. (A **FOREBODING** is the feeling that something is about to happen.) *(adj.)*

- ❑ The policeman's purple face and clenched fists **FOREBODE** his anger.

FORTE
(for TAY) *n.*
something in which a person excels

Link: **FORT**

*"Steve's **FORTE** is building tree **FORTS**."*

- ❑ Spelling has always been Zachary's **FORTE**.
- ❑ Tanya is a born actress, so the director highlighted her **FORTE** by giving her the lead in the play.
- ❑ Although he loved to play baseball, his **FORTE** is really golf.

Match the word with its definition.

___ 1. **exemplar**   a. to restrain; to hamper
___ 2. **exodus**   b. to predict or foretell
___ 3. **exonerate**   c. a mass departure
___ 4. **expatriate**   d. patience
___ 5. **extrude**   e. a model or original
___ 6. **fetter**   f. banish; leave one's country
___ 7. **fiasco**   g. a complete or humiliating failure
___ 8. **forbearance** h. to free from accusation or blame
___ 9. **forebode**   i. something in which a person excels
___ 10. **forte**   j. to force out through a small opening

Fill in the blanks with the most appropriate word.
The word form may need changing.

1. Toothpaste _____ from the tube when you squeeze it.

2. Charlie has always been an _____ student.

3. Spelling has always been Zachary's _____.

4. The prisoners were _____ by shackles around their ankles.

5. In ancient Greece it was believed that a sage could _____ the future.

6. There was an immediate _____ of people from the theater when someone yelled, "Fire!"

7. The hunter showed great _____ by sitting in the tree stand all day long.

8. The children's plan to release all the animals at the Humane Society was an utter _____.

9. When he was released from jail, he finally felt _____ of his crime.

10. Some American communists _____ to the Soviet Union during the Cold War.

157

FORTHRIGHT

(FORTH rite) *adj./n.*
directly forward; without hesitation;
a straight path

Link: **FOURTH FROM THE RIGHT**

*"The soldier **FOURTH FROM THE RIGHT** was **FORTHRIGHT**." (adj.)*

❑ Whenever I want a **FORTHRIGHT** opinion, I always ask my two-year-old son. *(adj.)*

❑ The boss asked everyone to be **FORTHRIGHT** at the company meeting. *(n.)*

❑ When Kathy asked Mark if her dress made her look fat, she wasn't expecting his answer to be so **FORTHRIGHT**. *(n.)*

FRANK

(frank) *adj.*
marked by free and sincere
expression

Link: **FRANKFURTER**

*"A **FRANK FRANKFURTER**"*

- ❏ Jim's **FRANK** remark about Marge's weight made her cry.

- ❏ The doctor was **FRANK** about Lisa's prognosis.

- ❏ The boss encouraged us to speak **FRANKLY** at the meeting. *(adv.)*

FRAY

(fray) *n.*
fight or scuffle; brawl

Link: **HAY**

"A FRAY in the HAY"

- ❑ The party turned into a **FRAY** when the bikers showed up.

- ❑ A **FRAY** occurred in the cafeteria when Kirk spilled his lunch on Jody.

- ❑ When Mark was beaned by the pitcher, a **FRAY** ensued between the teams.

FUSILLADE
(FYOO se lahd) *n.*
a rapid outburst or barrage

Link: **FUSELAGE**

*"The aircraft **FUSELAGE** received
a **FUSILLADE** of gunfire."*

- ❏ The soldier jumped behind a concrete wall for protection from the **FUSILLADE** of gunfire.

- ❏ The guard at the gate was surprised by a **FUSILLADE** of arrows which allowed the invaders to gain entrance to the castle.

- ❏ The defense lawyer overwhelmed the witness with a **FUSILLADE** of questions.

GAMBIT

(GAM bit) *v.*
to take a risk for some advantage

Link: **GAMBLE**

*"A **GAMBIT** not worth the **GAMBLE**"*

- ❑ The general's **GAMBIT** paid off when his troops won the battle.

- ❑ The chess player's **GAMBIT** was unsuccessful when he was put in checkmate.

- ❑ The employee's daring **GAMBIT** won him a raise from his boss.

GARNER
(GAHR nur) *v.*
to gather or store

Link: **GARDENER**

*"The **GARDENER GARNERED** a large crop."*

- ❑ Maria worked to **GARNER** all the information she could before she started writing her report.

- ❑ Throughout her lifetime, Bernice **GARNERED** enough antique furniture to fill five houses.

- ❑ Jonathan was guilty of **GARNERING** illegal information on the internet.

GASTRONOMY
(ga STRON uh mee) *n.*
the art of good eating;
culinary customs or style

Link: **ASTRONOMY**

*"Sam enjoyed **ASTRONOMY**, while
Big Bernard enjoyed **GASTRONOMY**."*

- ❑ One can learn a great deal about a country by studying its **GASTRONOMY**.

- ❑ French **GASTRONOMY** is distinguished by the use of wines and sauces.

- ❑ Toni developed her **GASTRONOMY** while attending culinary school.

GRADIENT
(GRAY dee unt) *n.*
a rate of inclination; a slope

Link: **GREAT AUNT**

*"It's tough getting a **GREAT AUNT**
up a steep **GRADIENT**."*

❑ The **GRADIENT** of the hill made it difficult to peddle my bike.

❑ The **GRADIENT** of metabolism is important in the field of biology.

❑ The teacher put the grades on a **GRADIENT** so that more students would do well on the hard test.

GRAVITY
(GRAV ih tee) *n.*
seriousness or importance

Link: **GRAVITY**

*"Sir Isaac Newton about to realize
the **GRAVITY** of **GRAVITY**"*

❑ Young children don't understand the **GRAVITY** of playing with matches until they burn themselves.

❑ The **GRAVITY** of the situation multiplied when Frank made the hole in the boat bigger while trying to patch it.

❑ We didn't realize the **GRAVITY** of Steven's drug addiction until it was too late.

GREGARIOUS
(gruh GAIR ee us) *adj.*
seeking and enjoying the
company of others; sociable

Link: **GREG HILARIOUS**

"GREGARIOUS GREG
was HILARIOUS."

❑ Paige was so **GREGARIOUS** she hated to be alone.

❑ Carol, to the contrary, was not **GREGARIOUS**. At parties she rarely talked with anyone.

❑ Bernard's **GREGARIOUS** nature made him an enjoyable person.

Match the word with its definition.

___ 1. **forthright**   a. a rate of inclination; a slope
___ 2. **frank**   b. a rapid outburst or barrage
___ 3. **fray**   c. seriousness or importance
___ 4. **fusillade**   d. the art of good eating
___ 5. **gambit**   e. free and sincere expression
___ 6. **garner**   f. to take a risk for some advantage
___ 7. **gastronomy**   g. fight or scuffle; brawl
___ 8. **gradient**   h. to gather or store
___ 9. **gravity**   i. directly forward; without hesitation
___ 10. **gregarious**   j. sociable

Fill in the blanks with the most appropriate word. The word form may need changing.

1. Maria worked to _____ all the information she could before she started writing her report.

2. The general's _____ paid off when his troops won the battle.

3. The _____ of the hill made it difficult to peddle my bike.

4. The party turned into a _____ when the bikers showed up.

5. The boss asked everyone to be _____ at the company meeting.

6. The doctor was _____ about Lisa's prognosis.

7. Young children don't understand the _____ of playing with matches until they burn themselves.

8. Bernard's _____ nature made him an enjoyable person.

9. The guard at the gate was surprised by a _____ of arrows which allowed the invaders to gain entrance to the castle.

10. One can learn a great deal about a country by studying its _____.

GULLIBLE
(GUL ih bul) *adj.*
easily cheated or fooled

Link: **GULL**

"A GULLIBLE GULL"

- ❏ Joel could not believe he had been so **GULLIBLE** as to believe his friend's wild story.

- ❏ Con artists rely on the **GULLIBILITY** of people to take money from their victims. *(n.)*

- ❏ The elderly woman **GULLIBLY** gave her credit card number to the man on the phone. *(adv.)*

HAMPER

(HAM pur) *v.*
to prevent the free movement, action,
or progress of; to hinder or impede

Link: **HAMPER**

*"A clothes **HAMPER HAMPERING** traffic"*

❑ His small stature **HAMPERED** Dan's chances of making the football team.

❑ Not routinely changing the car's oil will **HAMPER** its performance.

❑ A thunderstorm **HAMPERED** our plans of going to the beach.

HEARTEN

(HAHR tin) *v.*
to give strength, courage,
or hope; to encourage

Link: **HEART**

*"A **HEART** patient receiving
not so **HEARTENING** news"*

- ❏ The congregation received some **HEARTENING** words from their pastor.

- ❏ It was **HEARTENING** to receive so many cards from my friends when I was in the hospital.

- ❏ Our coach gave a **HEARTENED** speech that made us confident we would win the game.

HIATUS

(hye AY tus) *n.*
a gap or an interruption in space,
time, or continuity; a break

Link: **BETWEEN US**

*"A **HIATUS BETWEEN US**"*

- ❑ Emily looked to Christmas Break as a welcome **HIATUS** from the drudgery of school work.

- ❑ Susan asked for a three month **HIATUS** from work to spend time with her new baby.

- ❑ After reviewing the tax map, Richard found a **HIATUS** of ownership between his property and his neighbor's.

HIERARCHY

(HYE er ahr kee) *n.*
categorization of a group
according to ability or status

Link: **HIGH ARCH**

*"The **HIGH ARCH** of **HIERARCHY**"*

❑ Ed was very low on the company's **HIERARCHY**;
he only delivered the mail and emptied trash.

❑ Chief Sitting Bull was at the top of the tribe's
HIERARCHY.

❑ In the 1700s one's rank in the **HIERARCHY** of
noble birth often determined his wealth.

ICONOCLAST

(ahy KON oh klast) *n.*
one who attacks and seeks to overthrow
traditional or popular ideas or institutions

Link: **KIND TO THE PAST**

*"An **ICONOCLAST** not **KIND TO THE PAST**"*

❑ Steve Jobs was a great **ICONOCLAST** because
of his innovative contributions to the tech
industry.

❑ Young voters were attracted to the candidate's
ICONOCLASTIC platform. *(adj.)*

❑ Thomas Edison was a great **ICONOCLAST**;
without his **ICONOCLASTIC** views we might still
be sitting in the dark. *(n./adj.)*

IDOLATRY
(ahy DOLL ah tree) *n.*
blind or excessive devotion to something

Link: **DOLL TREE**

*"The twins' love of their **DOLL TREE**
bordered on **IDOLATRY**."*

❑ Ben's parents worried about his **IDOLATRY** to the occult.

❑ Elvis is the god of his **IDOLATRY**.

❑ Peter has an **IDOLATRY** for golf.

IDYLLIC

(ahy DIL ik) *adj.*

charming in a rustic way; naturally peaceful

Link: **DILL LICK**

"An IDYLLIC DILL LICK"

- ❑ Chuck and Cathy bought an **IDYLLIC** cabin in the Smoky Mountains.

- ❑ Our camping trip was **IDYLLIC**; we went for long hikes and didn't watch TV all weekend.

- ❑ Uncle Frank likes to paint **IDYLLIC** seascapes.

IMPAIR

(im PAIR) *v.*
to cause to diminish, as in
strength, value, or quality

Link: **PEAR**

*"An **IMPAIRED PEAR**"*

- ❑ A constant fast-food diet will eventually **IMPAIR** one's health.

- ❑ An overly aggressive negotiator can often **IMPAIR** negotiations.

- ❑ Our best soccer player was **IMPAIRED** when he hurt his knee.

INCESSANT
(in SES unt) *adj.*
continuing without interruption; nonstop

Link: **INSECTS AND ANTS**

*"INSECTS and ANTS are
INCESSANT picnic pests."*

❏ The teacher gave Allison and Karen a detention
for their **INCESSANT** chatter in class.

❏ The **INCESSANT** rain flooded the front yard.

❏ Their **INCESSANT** bickering drove Mike and
Barbara to divorce.

VOCABULARY CARTOONS Review #15

Match the word with its definition.

___ 1. **gullible** a. a gap
___ 2. **hamper** b. one who attacks popular ideas
___ 3. **hearten** c. nonstop
___ 4. **hiatus** d. easily cheated or fooled
___ 5. **hierarchy** e. a group according to ability
___ 6. **iconoclast** f. to diminish, as in strength
___ 7. **idolatry** g. to give strength
___ 8. **idyllic** h. excessive devotion to
___ 9. **impair** i. something naturally peaceful
___ 10. **incessant** j. to hinder or impede

Fill in the blanks with the most appropriate word. The word form may need changing.

1. Emily looked to Christmas Break as a welcome _____ from the drudgery of school work.

2. The teacher gave Allison and Karen a detention for their _____ chatter in class.

3. A thunderstorm _____ our plans of going to the beach.

4. Young voters were attracted to the candidate's _____ platform.

5. Ed was very low on the company's _____ ; he only delivered the mail and emptied trash.

6. The congregation received some _____ words from their pastor.

7. Ben's parents worried about his _____ to the occult.

8. Joel could not believe he had been so _____ as to believe his friend's wild story.

9. A constant fast-food diet will eventually _____ one's health.

10. Chuck and Cathy bought an _____ cabin in the Smoky Mountains.

179

INCONTROVERTIBLE

(in kon trah VUR tih bul) *adj.*
not able to be "turned against" or
disputed; certain; indisputable

Link: **CONVERTIBLE**

*"It's **INCONTROVERTIBLE** that beauty
queens ride in **CONVERTIBLES**."*

❑ The suspect's fingerprints on the window were
considered **INCONTROVERTIBLE** evidence of
his participation in the robbery.

❑ Christina **INCONTROVERTIBLY** believes in
herself. (*adv.*)

❑ It is **INCONTROVERTIBLE** that two plus two
equals four.

INDOLENCE
(IN doh lents) *n.*
inclination to laziness

Link: **ON THE FENCE**

*"The crows sat with **INDOLENCE**
ON THE FENCE."*

❑ Christopher may get by in high school, but college professors will never put up with such **INDOLENCE**.

❑ Sara was fired from her job because of her **INDOLENCE**.

❑ Because his parents are such hard workers, Brad's **INDOLENCE** in school came as a shock to them.

INFLUX

(IN fluks) *n.*
a mass arrival or incoming;
a continuous coming

Link: **TRUCKS**

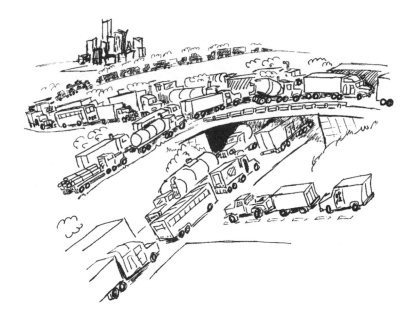

*"An **INFLUX** of **TRUCKS**"*

- ❑ South Florida has an **INFLUX** of northern tourists every winter.

- ❑ The **INFLUX** of peoples of other countries during the seventeenth and eighteenth centuries is what made America a melting pot.

- ❑ We will have to build an addition on to the school because of the **INFLUX** of new students.

INTREPID
(in TREP id) *adj.*
fearless; bold

Link: **TRIP ED**

*"Everyone considered David **INTREPID** after he **TRIPPED ED**, the bully, in the cafeteria."*

❏ The **INTREPID** bullfighter stood in the arena before the fierce bull.

❏ Ed **INTREPIDLY** opened the hatch of the plane as he prepared for his first jump. *(adv.)*

❏ The Green Berets have always been known for their **INTREPIDITY**. *(n.)*

INUNDATE

(IN un dayt) *v.*
to overwhelm with
abundance or excess; flood

Link: **IAN'S DATE**

"IAN was INUNDATED with DATES."

- ❑ After the rains, the fields were **INUNDATED** with water.

- ❑ During final exams, we are so **INUNDATED** with school work that we have no time for fun.

- ❑ Jack's father used to **INUNDATE** the front yard in the winter so all his friends could ice skate.

INURE

(in YOOR) *v.*
to get used to something
undesirable; harden

Link: **MANURE**

*"Shoveling **MANURE** takes awhile to **INURE**."*

- ❑ The prisoner became **INURED** to his new life in prison.

- ❑ After thirty days at sea, Bob was **INURED** to life in a life raft.

- ❑ The substitute teacher was unable to **INURE** himself to some of the students.

JAUNT
(jawnt) *n.*
a short pleasure trip

Link: **HAUNT**

*"A **HAUNTED JAUNT**"*

- ❑ After not taking a family vacation for two years, a **JAUNT** to the beach was a pleasant respite.

- ❑ My parents are always taking **JAUNTS** in their new motor home.

- ❑ Mary and Bryan always enjoy their annual **JAUNT** to the mountains.

JETSAM
(JET sem) *n.*
cargo or equipment thrown
overboard to lighten an imperiled
vessel; discarded odds and ends

Link: **JETS**

*"The **JETS** became **JETSAM**."*

❑ After the ship sank, the crew clung to any floating
JETSAM they could find.

❑ Jessica found a piece of blue glass on the water's
edge, but her father explained it was merely
JETSAM.

❑ After a storm, **JETSAM** is often discovered on the
beach.

KINDLE

(KIN dl) *v.*
to cause to burn or ignite;
to arouse or inspire

Link: **CANDLE**

*"Patrick found a unique way
to **KINDLE CANDLES**."*

- ❑ Because Christine once had feelings for him, Joe thought sending flowers might again **KINDLE** her affections.

- ❑ It is difficult to **KINDLE** a fire with damp fire wood.

- ❑ The fire **KINDLED** when he squirted on some lighter fluid.

Link: **KISS ME**

*"**KISS ME** baby, it's **KISMET**."*

❑ The happy couple attributed the success of their relationship to **KISMET**.

❑ To those who believe in fate, **KISMET** is the cause of everything.

❑ It was **KISMET** that they both returned to their old high school on the same day twenty years after graduation.

Match the word with its definition.

__	1. **incontrovertible**	a. to overwhelm with abundance
__	2. **indolence**	b. not able to be disputed
__	3. **influx**	c. a short pleasure trip
__	4. **intrepid**	d. cargo thrown overboard
__	5. **inundate**	e. to get used to something
__	6. **inure**	f. to cause to burn or ignite
__	7. **jaunt**	g. a mass arrival
__	8. **jetsam**	h. inclination to laziness
__	9. **kindle**	i. fate
__	10. **kismet**	j. fearless; bold

Fill in the blanks with the most appropriate word. The word form may need changing.

1. My parents are always taking _____ in their new motor home.

2. Sara was fired from her job because of her _____.

3. It is difficult to _____ a fire with damp fire wood.

4. The suspect's fingerprints on the window were considered _____ evidence of his participation in the robbery.

5. The happy couple attributed the success of their relationship to _____.

6. South Florida has an _____ of northern tourists every winter.

7. After the ship sank, the crew clung to any floating _____ they could find.

8. The _____ bullfighter stood in the arena before the fierce bull.

9. After the rains, the fields were _____ with water.

10. The prisoner became _____ to his new life in prison.

LACKADAISICAL
(lak ah DAY zi kul) *adj.*
showing lack of interest; listless

Link: **YAK IN THE DAISIES**

*"A **LACKADAISICAL YAK IN THE DAISIES**"*

- ❑ Margaret's **LACKADAISICAL** attitude will hurt her chances of getting into college.

- ❑ He just stood there **LACKADAISICALLY** staring into space. *(adv.)*

- ❑ I would not want to go to a doctor who had a **LACKADAISICAL** approach to his practice.

LAMBASTE
(lam BAYST) *v.*
to give a thrashing; to assault violently

Link: **LAMB**

*"The **LAMB** took a **LAMBASTING**
from the champ."*

❑ The drill sergeant **LAMBASTED** his troops for their poor performance on the obstacle course.

❑ George received a verbal **LAMBASTING** from his father for not doing his chores.

❑ The fierce storm **LAMBASTED** the ship and its crew.

LAMPOON

(lam POON) *n./v.*
light, good-humored satire;
to make the subject of satire

Link: **HARPOON**

*"A **LAMPOON** with a **HARPOON**"* (n.)

❑ The president took no offense to the **LAMPOON** of him on the comedy show, he actually thought it was funny. *(n.)*

❑ When the boss leaves the office, Sylvester always **LAMPOONS** the poor man's shortcomings. *(v.)*

❑ *MAD* magazine **LAMPOONS** many aspects of American culture. *(v.)*

LANGUID

(LANG gwid) *adj.*
lacking energy; weak; showing
little interest in anything

Link: **SQUID**

*"A **LANGUID SQUID**"*

❑ After his bout with the flu, Joe was **LANGUID**
  and unable to workout for over a week.

❑ Jill finished the triathlon, but at the finish line she
  LANGUIDLY sank to the ground. *(adv.)*

❑ The teacher's **LANGUID** approach to American
  History did not motivate the class.

LATENT
(LAYT nt) *adj.*
lying hidden or undeveloped; potential

Link: **LAY TENT**

*"Never **LAY** your **TENT** on a **LATENT** volcano."*

❑ Trent had a **LATENT** talent as a singer which he didn't discover until he was in his 50s.

❑ Because the disease was in a **LATENT** state, no one knew she was ill.

❑ Jeri's parents were unaware of her **LATENT** desire to study law and to become an attorney.

LITHE

(lythe) *adj.*
bending easily and gracefully

Link: **LIZA**

THAT'S LIZA,
THE MOST LITHE
GYMNAST
ON THE TEAM.

*"**LIZA** is the most **LITHE** gymnast on our team."*

- ❑ The **LITHE** ballerina stretched her muscles before her performance.

- ❑ The **LITHE** gymnast dismounted without a sound.

- ❑ The dancer was as **LITHE** as a cat as he leapt across the stage.

LOGISTICS
(loh JIS tiks) *n.*
the management of the details
of an operation

Link: **LOGS AND STICKS**

*"Lumber mill **LOGISTICS** consist
of **LOGS AND STICKS**."*

❑ The Normandy invasion is a great example of
military **LOGISTICS**.

❑ The **LOGISTICS** involved in building the Golden
Gate Bridge required an immense amount of time
and resources.

❑ General Eisenhower was an expert of military
LOGISTICS.

MALADROIT

(mal uh DROYT) *adj.*
clumsy; inept

Link: **DRAW IT**

*"The **MALADROIT** artist couldn't **DRAW IT**."*

- ❑ The **MALADROIT** painter spilled a can of paint on our new carpet.

- ❑ Actor Charlie Chaplin, was famous for his **MALADROIT** roles.

- ❑ Bob was upset with the mechanic's **MALADROIT** attempt to repair his car.

MALAISE
(ma LAYZ) *n.*
a vague feeling of bodily discomfort,
as at the beginning of an illness

Link: **MAYONNAISE**

*"Hal's **MALAISE** was brought on
by spoiled **MAYONNAISE**."*

- ❑ Samantha's **MALAISE** was later diagnosed as food poisoning.

- ❑ Beth's **MALAISE** began when she awoke with a sore throat.

- ❑ A sudden **MALAISE** overcame Jonathan when the postman delivered a certified letter from the IRS.

MALCONTENT

(mal kon TENT) *adj./n.*
dissatisfied with existing conditions;
an unhappy person

Link: **CONTENT**

*"Once a **MALCONTENT**, the prisoner was
now **CONTENT** with his living conditions." (n.)*

❑ The **MALCONTENT** workers decided to strike
against the company's labor policies. *(adj.)*

❑ We seem to always have one **MALCONTENT** in
the group who eventually brings everyone down.
(n.)

❑ The **MALCONTENT** little boy finally smiled when
his mother gave him an ice-cream cone. *(adj.)*

VOCABULARY CARTOONS Review #17

Match the word with its definition.

___	1. **lackadaisical**	a.	bending easily and gracefully
___	2. **lambaste**	b.	management of the details
___	3. **lampoon**	c.	to give a thrashing
___	4. **languid**	d.	light, good-humored satire
___	5. **latent**	e.	showing lack of interest
___	6. **lithe**	f.	a vague feeling of discomfort
___	7. **logistics**	g.	lacking energy
___	8. **maladroit**	h.	dissatisfied with existing conditions
___	9. **malaise**	i.	clumsy; inept
___	10. **malcontent**	j.	laying hidden

Fill in the blanks with the most appropriate word.
The word form may need changing.

1. The _____ workers decided to strike against the company's labor policies.

2. Margaret's _____ attitude will hurt her chances of getting into college.

3. After his bout with the flu, Joe was _____ and unable to workout for over a week.

4. Samantha's _____ was later diagnosed as food poisoning.

5. The drill sergeant _____ his troops for their poor performance on the obstacle course.

6. The president took no offense to the _____ of him on the comedy show, he actually thought it was funny.

7. The _____ painter spilled a can of paint on our new carpet.

8. The _____ involved in building the Golden Gate Bridge required an immense amount of time and resources.

9. The _____ ballerina stretched her muscles before her performance.

10. Trent had a _____ talent as a singer which he didn't discover until he was in his 50s.

201

MALICE
(MAL is) *n.*
a desire or intention to harm
others or see them suffer

Link: **ALICE**

*"**ALICE** has **MALICE** towards
door to door salesmen."*

❏ The prisoner was not granted parole because
his **MALICE** was still obvious.

❏ Our government is based on justice, with
MALICE toward none.

❏ We could not believe that such a young girl
could harbor such **MALICE** toward her
neighbors.

MALODOR
(mal OH dor) *n.*
a bad odor

Link: **BAD ODOR**

*"Barnyard **MALODOR** means
barnyard **BAD ODOR**."*

- ❑ After the storm, the **MALODOR** made it clear that the sewers were not working.

- ❑ A **MALODOROUS** stench filled the car after we ran over the skunk. *(adj.)*

- ❑ The **MALODOR** of the stray dog kept us at arm's length.

MAMMOTH
(MAM uth) *adj.*
huge; gigantic

Link: **MOTH**

*"A **MAMMOTH MOTH**"*

- ❑ Until I visited Manhattan, I could not imagine the **MAMMOTH** size of the Empire State Building.

- ❑ Herman Melville's title character, Moby Dick, is a **MAMMOTH** whale.

- ❑ When Jane returned from vacation, she found a **MAMMOTH** amount of work piled on her desk.

MANIFEST
(MAN ih fest) *v.*
to make clear or evident to the eye; obvious

Link: **MAN IN VEST**

*"The **MAN IN THE VEST**
MANIFESTED that he is a butler."*

❑ Rebecca's flu symptoms **MANIFESTED** by a
runny nose and high fever.

❑ Larry **MANIFESTED** his intentions to propose by
kneeling on one knee and presenting Mary with a
diamond ring.

❑ Ryan **MANIFESTED** a sense of urgency when he
discovered he was already 30 minutes late for his
appointment.

MARITIME

(MARE ih time) *adj.*
near the sea; concerned with
navigation or commerce on the sea

Link: **MERRY TIME**

*"The **MARITIME** sailors are
having a **MERRY TIME**."*

❑ While in our nation's capitol, we visited the
MARITIME War Museum.

❑ Rick's desire is to become a **MARITIME** lawyer.

❑ Boston is a famous **MARITIME** city.

MAWKISH

(MAW kish) *adj.*
excessively and
objectionably sentimental

Link: **MA'S KISS**

*"**MA'S KISS** can be **MAWKISH**."*

- Elizabeth is so **MAWKISH** that she cries at every wedding.

- Steve doesn't care for **MAWKISH** birthday cards; he likes funny ones instead.

- The bride's **MAWKISH** behavior embarrassed the groom.

METE

(MEET) *v.*
to distribute by or as if
by measure; to allot

Link: **MEAT**

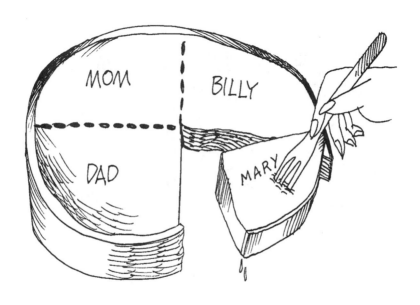

*"Mom always **METES** out the **MEAT**."*

❑ Allison stood in the doorway in a witch costume
   and **METED** out Halloween candy to all the kids.

❑ The volunteer fireman **METED** out sandbags to
   all worried homeowners.

❑ The sergeant **METED** out ammunition to all
   soldiers in the platoon.

MOGUL
(MOH guhl) *n.*
a very rich or powerful
person; a magnate

Link: **SEA GULL**

*"A **SEA GULL MOGUL**"*

❑ Howard Hughes was a famous **MOGUL** who was rarely seen in public.

❑ Leslie's dream is to marry a **MOGUL**, have ten kids, and live in luxury.

❑ After forming Microsoft, Bill Gates became the most recognized computer **MOGUL**.

MORASS

(muh RASS) *n.*
anything that hinders, traps or
overwhelms; low-lying, soggy ground

Link: **MOLASSES**

*"The **MOLASSES** created a **MORASS**."*

❑ The **MORASS** surrounding the castle was
ineffective during the dry season.

❑ The jeep sank deep into the **MORASS** and could
go no further.

❑ The **MORASS** was too wet for gardening so we
brought in some fill dirt.

MOTTLE

(MOT ul) *v./adj.*
to mark with spots or blotches of different
shades or colors; marked with spots

Link: **BOTTLE**

*"The rare **MOTTLED** mouse
caught in a **BOTTLE**" (adj.)*

- ❏ The Dalmatian's **MOTTLED** coat is its salient trait. *(adj.)*

- ❏ Chicken pox **MOTTLED** the boy's skin with lesions. *(v.)*

- ❏ The soldier's **MOTTLED** uniform was designed for camouflage. *(adj.)*

Match the word with its definition.

___ 1. **malice**	a.	to distribute by or as if by measure
___ 2. **malodor**	b.	concerned with the sea
___ 3. **mammoth**	c.	a bad odor
___ 4. **manifest**	d.	anything that hinders
___ 5. **maritime**	e.	huge; gigantic
___ 6. **mawkish**	f.	excessively sentimental
___ 7. **mete**	g.	a desire to harm others
___ 8. **mogul**	h.	to mark with spots
___ 9. **morass**	i.	to make clear
___ 10. **mottle**	j.	a very rich or powerful person

**Fill in the blanks with the most appropriate word.
The word form may need changing.**

1. Steve doesn't care for _____ birthday cards; he likes funny ones instead.

2. Allison stood in the doorway in a witch costume and _____ out Halloween candy to all the kids.

3. Until I visited Manhattan, I could not imagine the _____ size of the Empire State Building.

4. After the storm, the _____ made it clear that the sewers were not working.

5. The prisoner was not granted parole because his _____ was still obvious.

6. Howard Hughes was a famous _____ who was rarely seen in public.

7. Rebecca's flu symptoms _____ by a runny nose and high fever.

8. Chicken pox _____ the boy's skin with lesions.

9. Boston is a famous _____ city.

10. The jeep sank deep into the _____ and could go no further.

NEMESIS

(NEM eh sis) *n.*
an opponent that cannot
be beaten or overcome

Link: **MY SIS**

"My NEMESIS is MY SIS."

- ❑ Lex Luther considers Superman his **NEMESIS**.

- ❑ Tom is my **NEMESIS** because I can beat every-one who beats him in tennis, but I can't beat him.

- ❑ Potato chips are Paul's **NEMESIS**; if he takes one bite he can't stop eating them.

NETTLE
(NET ul) *v.*
to irritate; vex

Link: **SETTLE**

*"Mosquitoes **NETTLE** when they **SETTLE**."*

- ❑ My little brother always seems to **NETTLE** me.
- ❑ Hip Hop music **NETTLES** my parents.
- ❑ The squeaky ceiling fan **NETTLED** me all night long.

NOCTURNAL
(nawk TUR nul) *adj.*
of or occurring at night

Link: **NIGHT TURTLE**

"A NOCTURNAL TURTLE"

- ❑ **NOCTURNAL** animals sleep during the day and are active at night.

- ❑ A **NOCTURNAL** person is one who stays up late at night.

- ❑ **DIURNAL**, which means of or occurring during the day, is the opposite of **NOCTURNAL**.

NULLIFY
(NUL ih fye) *v.*
to make useless; cancel; undo

Link: **FLY**

"How to NULLIFY a FLY."

- ❑ Christopher said his agreement to play for the Cowboys had been **NULLIFIED** due to his injury.

- ❑ The purchase contract could be **NULLIFIED** because it had never been signed by the buyer.

- ❑ The contract had a 30 day guarantee, therefore it could be **NULLIFIED** within that period.

NURTURE

(NUR chur) *v.*
to nourish, to feed; to
educate; to train; to foster

Link: **NURSE**

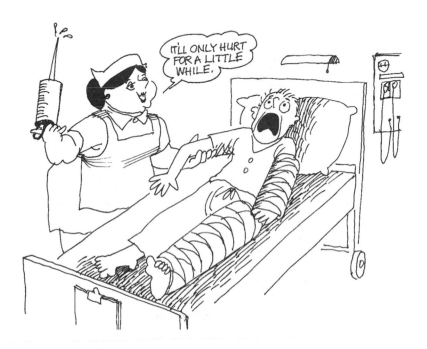

"NURSES NURTURE the sick and ailing."

❑ Mother birds **NURTURE** their young.

❑ Laura **NURTURED** the abandoned puppy and kept him as her own.

❑ During her first year of college, Elizabeth often called her mother for some **NURTURING** words. *(adj.)*

OBESE

(oh BEES) *adj.*
extremely fat; grossly overweight

Link: **BEES**

"OBESE BEES"

- ❑ Frederick was so **OBESE** he could not fit through the door.

- ❑ **OBESITY** is a problem caused by lack of exercise, poor diet control, and metabolism. *(n.)*

- ❑ **OBESE** people are frequently on diets all their lives.

OBTRUDE
(uhb TROOD) *v.*
to impose oneself or one's
ideas on others; to stick out

Link: **NUDE**

*"Ernie hated to **OBTRUDE** in the **NUDE**,
but this was an emergency."*

- ❏ Dad always liked to **OBTRUDE** his ideas upon others.

- ❏ Tanya hoped her parents wouldn't **OBTRUDE** upon her wedding plans.

- ❏ Tina's **OBTRUSIVE** personality made it hard for her to make friends. *(adj.)*

OFFAL

(AW full) *n.*
waste parts, especially of a
butchered animal; rubbish

Link: **AWFUL**

*"The **OFFAL** smelled **AWFUL**."*

- ❑ The dog rooted through the **OFFAL** for scraps of food.

- ❑ The young cheetah left the **OFFAL** of his prey to the buzzards.

- ❑ The butcher saved the **OFFAL** for his dogs.

OFFICIOUS

(uh FISH us) *adj.*
interfering; intrusive; eager in offering
unwanted services or advice

Link: **OFFICE**

*"An **OFFICIOUS OFFICE** helper"*

❑ Uncle Dan was so **OFFICIOUS** that he wanted to help me work on my antique cars, even though he knew nothing about engines.

❑ The **OFFICIOUS** waitress would not go away, even when Jennifer told her that she wanted only coffee.

❑ Ralph's **OFFICIOUSNESS** was an attempt to make friends which usually backfired on him. *(n.)*

ONEROUS

(AHN ur us) *adj.*
troublesome or oppressive; burdensome

Link: **OWNER**

*"A pet shop OWNER'S life
can become ONEROUS."*

___

❏ Our platoon was given the **ONEROUS** duty of charging up a well-defended hill.

❏ After our truck ran out of gas, we had the **ONEROUS** task of pushing it two miles to the nearest gas station.

❏ The teacher was given a classroom aide because her class was so **ONEROUS**.

VOCABULARY CARTOONS Review #19

Match the word with its definition.

__	1. **nemesis**	a.	to make useless; cancel; undo
__	2. **nettle**	b.	extremely fat
__	3. **nocturnal**	c.	an opponent difficult to beat
__	4. **nullify**	d.	troublesome or oppressive
__	5. **nurture**	e.	waste parts
__	6. **obese**	f.	of or occurring at night
__	7. **obtrude**	g.	to nourish, to feed; to train; to foster
__	8. **offal**	h.	to irritate; vex
__	9. **officious**	i.	eager in offering unwanted advice
__	10. **onerous**	j.	to stick out

Fill in the blanks with the most appropriate word. The word form may need changing.

1. Frederick was so _____ he could not fit through the door.

2. Mother birds _____ their young.

3. Tanya hoped her parents wouldn't _____ upon her wedding plans.

4. _____ animals sleep during the day and are active at night.

5. Our platoon was given the _____ duty of charging up a well-defended hill.

6. Hip Hop music _____ my parents.

7. Lex Luther considers Superman his _____.

8. The purchase contract could be _____ because it had never been signed by the buyer.

9. The _____ waitress would not go away even when Jennifer told her that she wanted only coffee.

10. The dog rooted through the _____ for scraps of food.

OPAQUE

(oh PAYK) *adj.*
impervious to light; dull; hard
to understand; unclear

Link: **FAKE**

"This "diamond" is OPAQUE;
it must be FAKE."

❑ Jean put an **OPAQUE** blue glaze on her ceramic teapot.

❑ The old dishwashing machine left the water glasses with an **OPAQUE** finish.

❑ The problem remains **OPAQUE** despite explanation.

OSTENSIBLE

(ah STEN suh bul) *adj.*
appearing as such; offered
as genuine or real

Link: **SENSIBLE**

*"Taking an **OSTENSIBLE** short-cut is
not always the **SENSIBLE** thing to do."*

- Her **OSTENSIBLE** purpose was borrowing sugar, but she really wanted to see the new furniture.

- The **OSTENSIBLE** reason that Sam became a member of the golf club was to play golf, but he really wanted to meet more potential clients.

- Madison **OSTENSIBLY** goes to the gym to work out, she really likes to talk to all cute guys. *(adv.)*

PACIFIST

(PAS ih fist) *n.*
one who is in opposition
of war or violence

Link: **FIST**

*"A **PACIFIST** never uses his **FIST**."*

- ❑ Julie is such a **PACIFIST**; she doesn't even like violent movies.

- ❑ The **PACIFISTS** protested the boxing match by lying on the mat and refusing to move.

- ❑ Because of Brad's **PACIFISTIC** personality, he refused to get into a fight. *(adj.)*

PALISADE

(pal ih SAYD) *n.*
a fortification of timbers set in
the ground; an extended cliff

Link: **PAL IN THE SHADE**

MY PAL IS IN THE SHADE OF THE PALISADE.

MY PAL IS STILL IN THE SHADE OF THE PALISADE.

*"My PAL IN THE SHADE prefers
to sit under the PALISADES."*

❏ The king built a **PALISADE** to fortify his castle.

❏ The **PALISADES** of the Grand Canyon are a
natural beauty one must visit to appreciate.

❏ The **PALISADE** followed coastline, casting a
shadow across the beach.

PALLIATE
(PAL ee ayt) *v.*
to make seem less serious; to mitigate

Link: **PAL HE ATE**

"WAS IT YOUR PAL I ATE?"

*"The crocodile tried to **PALLIATE** his guilt for the duck's **PAL HE ATE**."*

- ❏ Christopher was given aspirin to **PALLIATE** his headache.

- ❏ After Alex's goldfish died, his mother bought him a puppy to **PALLIATE** his grief.

- ❏ The nurse **PALLIATED** the patient's burns by applying cold, wet bandages to the sensitive area.

PALPABLE
(PAL pah bul) *adj.*
capable of being touched or felt

Link: **PAL THE BULL**

"Our PAL, THE BULL, is PALPABLE."

- ❏ The **PALPABLE** imagery helps make the poem more realistic.

- ❏ The answer is as **PALPABLE** as the nose on your face.

- ❏ Fear ran **PALPABLY** through the crowd as the man wielded a pistol. *(adv.)*

PANACHE
(puh NASH) *n.*
dashing elegance of manner or style

Link: **MUSTACHE**

*"Sir Charles' **MUSTACHE** is a symbol of his **PANACHE**."*

- ❑ Eric entered the room with **PANACHE**, wearing his new tux, Rolex watch, and $500 shoes.

- ❑ It was evident by the woman's **PANACHE** that she was a member of the royal family.

- ❑ Mom was impressed with my **PANACHE** after I returned home from finishing school.

PANDEMIC
(pan DEM ik) *adj.*
widespread; general

Link: **PANDA**

*"**PANDAS** are **PANDEMIC** to China."*

- ❑ AIDS has spread in **PANDEMIC** proportions around the world.

- ❑ Disco's **PANDEMIC** popularity was short-lived in the 1970s.

- ❑ Boating is a **PANDEMIC** form of outdoor recreation in Florida.

PANORAMA
(pan uh RAM uh) *n.*
an unbroken view of a wide area

Link: **CAMERA**

*"A **CAMERA** for the **PANORAMA**"*

❑ We enjoyed the scenic **PANORAMA** while taking a hot air balloon ride.

❑ The **PANORAMA** from the top of the Empire State Building was spectacular.

❑ The Grand Canyon offers **PANORAMIC** views of great splendor. *(adj.)*

PARABLE
(PAIR ah bul) *n.*
a simple story illustrating a
moral or religious lesson

Link: **PAIR OF BULLS**

*"A **PAIR OF BULLS** reading a **PARABLE**"*

❏ My son's favorite book is one full of **PARABLES**.

❏ The story of the boy who cried wolf is a
   PARABLE about the consequences of telling
   lies.

❏ John's favorite part of Sunday school is when
   the teacher reads a **PARABLE**.

Match the word with its definition.

__	1. **opaque**	a.	appearing as such
__	2. **ostensible**	b.	to make seem less serious
__	3. **pacifist**	c.	widespread
__	4. **palisade**	d.	someone opposed to violence
__	5. **palliate**	e.	a moral or religious story
__	6. **palpable**	f.	a view of a wide area
__	7. **panache**	g.	impervious to light; unclear
__	8. **pandemic**	h.	dashing elegance
__	9. **panorama**	i.	a fortification; an extended cliff
__	10. **parable**	j.	capable of being touched or felt

Fill in the blanks with the most appropriate word.
The word form may need changing.

1. Christopher was given aspirin to _____ his headache.

2. The _____ protested the boxing match by lying on the mat and refusing to move.

3. My son's favorite book is one full of _____.

4. Jean put an _____ blue glaze on her ceramic teapot.

5. The answer is as _____ as the nose on your face.

6. The _____ reason that Sam became a member of the golf club was to play golf, but he really wanted to meet more potential clients.

7. The _____ from the top of the Empire State Building was spectacular.

8. The _____ followed coastline, casting a shadow across the beach.

9. AIDS has spread in _____ proportions around the world.

10. Eric entered the room with _____ , wearing his new tux, Rolex watch, and $500 shoes.

234

PARADIGM
(PAIR ah dime) *n.*
a pattern that serves
as a model or example

Link: **PAIR OF DIMES**

*"A **PARADIGM** of the new*
PAIR OF DIMES"

- ❑ Michael Jordan is a **PARADIGM** of a professional basketball player.

- ❑ When designing the Luxor Hotel in Las Vegas the architects used the Great Pyramids in Egypt as their **PARADIGM**.

- ❑ The Model-T was used as a **PARADIGM** by many automobile manufacturers in the early 1900s.

PARAGON
(PAIR ah gone) *n.*
a model or pattern of excellence

Link: **PAIR OF GUNS**

"A PARAGON PAIR OF GUNS"

❑ Although Joyce was a **PARAGON** of virtue, she was also good fun to be with at the same time.

❑ While not an architectural **PARAGON** to be copied, the sturdy old brick house has withstood many hurricanes.

❑ William named his shoe company **PARAGON** Shoes, with expectations customers would think his shoes the best.

PARLEY

(PAHR lee) *n.*
a conference, especially
between enemies

Link: **PARTY**

*"The **PARLEY** turned into a **PARTY**."*

- ❑ A **PARLEY** was scheduled between the leaders of the opposing nations.

- ❑ The National Football League owners and players **PARLEYED** to reach a settlement of salary caps. *(v.)*

- ❑ After a brief **PARLEY**, the defense attorney and prosecuting attorney agreed to settle the dispute out of court.

PATRIARCH
(PAY tree ahrk) *n.*
the leader of a family or tribe

Link: **PASTRY ART**

*"The **PATRIARCH'S** specialty is **PASTRY ART**."*

- ❑ Abraham is considered one of the **PATRIARCHS** of the Hebrew religion.

- ❑ William Bradford led the pilgrims to the new world and acted as **PATRIARCH** of the colony.

- ❑ The **PATRIARCH** is the one the tribe turns to for leadership and guidance.

PATRIMONY

(PA trih moh nee) *n.*
an inheritance from a father or an
ancestor; anything inherited

Link: **PAT'S MONEY**

*"**PAT'S MONEY** is his **PATRIMONY**."*

❑ My mother says my overly large nose is a result of
PATRIMONY since her family all have small
noses.

❑ Ill-will in the family was a result of arguing over the
PATRIMONY.

❑ Jonathan squandered his **PATRIMONY** and died
penniless.

PECCADILLO
(pek ah DIL oh) *n.*
a slight or trifling sin; a minor offense

Link: **ARMADILLO**

"Norm thought running over an
***ARMADILLO** was a **PECCADILLO**."*

❏ The reporters were more interested in the
president's personal **PECCADILLOES** than the
state of the economy.

❏ Being ticketed for running a red light is a mere
PECCADILLO compared to driving while
intoxicated.

❏ Bob couldn't believe he could be punished for
the **PECCADILLO** of not cleaning his room at
boarding school.

PECUNIARY
(pi KYOO nee er ee) *adj.*
consisting of or relating to money

Link: **PECULIAR DAIRY**

*"A **PECUNIARY PECULIAR DAIRY**"*

- ❑ Alex's concerns about college were specifically **PECUNIARY**.

- ❑ Ryan wanted to take Jessie to the prom but didn't ask her because of his **PECUNIARY** problems.

- ❑ **PECUNIARY** troubles are the primary reason for many failed marriages.

PEDESTRIAN
(peh DES tree ahn) *adj.*
ordinary; moving on foot

Link: **PEDESTRIAN**

"PEDESTRIAN PEDESTRIANS"

- ❑ The **PEDESTRIAN** crosswalk is marked by white lines running across the street.

- ❑ For once, can't we do something that isn't so boringly **PEDESTRIAN**?

- ❑ The right frame can make a **PEDESTRIAN** painting look like a million bucks.

PERPENDICULAR

(pur pen DIK yu ler) *adj.*
upright or vertical; being at right
angles to the plane of the horizon

Link: **PEN**

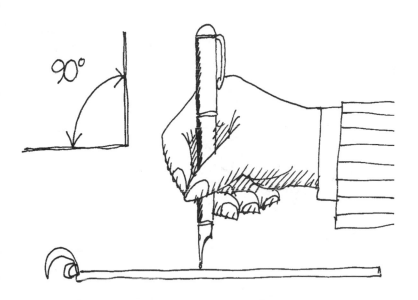

*"The **PEN** is **PERPENDICULAR**
to the pad of paper."*

- ☐ The pole is **PERPENDICULAR** to the ground.
- ☐ The tall mast of the sailing ship was built **PERPENDICULAR** to the deck.
- ☐ Because the wall was not **PERPENDICULAR**, it gradually succumbed to gravity and fell over.

PERSONIFY

(per SAWN ih fye) *v.*
to think of or represent as having
human qualities; to typify

Link: **PERSON FLY**

*"Captain Minerich is a **PERSON** who
PERSONIFIES FLYING."*

❏ Their child **PERSONIFIES** every thing that is good
about each of them.

❏ In her poem she attempts to **PERSONIFY** death.

❏ Benjamin Franklin **PERSONIFIES** all the
attributes of the Revolutionary period.

VOCABULARY CARTOONS Review #21

Match the word with its definition.

__	1. **paradigm**	a.	consisting of or relating to money
__	2. **paragon**	b.	a minor offense
__	3. **parley**	c.	a pattern that serves as a model
__	4. **patriarch**	d.	moving on foot
__	5. **patrimony**	e.	to think of as having human qualities
__	6. **peccadillo**	f.	an inheritance
__	7. **pecuniary**	g.	a conference between enemies
__	8. **pedestrian**	h.	a model or pattern of excellence
__	9. **perpendicular**	i.	the leader of a family or tribe
__	10. **personify**	j.	being at right angles

Fill in the blanks with the most appropriate word. The word form may need changing.

1. Although Joyce was a _____ of virtue, she was also good fun to be with at the same time.

2. Michael Jordan is a _____ of a professional basketball player.

3. _____ troubles are the primary reason for many failed marriages.

4. William Bradford led the pilgrims to the new world and acted as _____ of the colony.

5. The pole is _____ to the ground.

6. A _____ was scheduled between the leaders of the opposing nations.

7. In her poem she attempts to _____ death.

8. Jonathan squandered his _____ and died penniless.

9. Bob couldn't believe he could be punished for the _____ of not cleaning his room at boarding school.

10. The _____ crosswalk is marked by white lines running across the street.

245

PHILIPPIC

(fe LIP ik) *n.*
a verbal denunciation characterized
by harsh, insulting language; a tirade

Link: **FLIP IT**

*"The cook unleashed a **PHILIPPIC** when
his new helper couldn't **FLIP IT**."*

- ❑ The coach, in seeking to rouse the team,
  pronounced bitter **PHILIPPICS** against the
  opposing team.

- ❑ Rachel unleashed a **PHILIPPIC** when her
  brother broke her bike.

- ❑ Dad always directed **PHILIPPICS** at me
  whenever I got a bad grade.

PINGUID
(PEN gwed) *adj.*
fat

Link: **PENGUIN**

*"A **PINGUID PENGUIN**"*

- ☐ The **PINGUID** egg roll left a greasy stain on the paper plate.

- ☐ Mom served a **PINGUID** turkey for Thanksgiving dinner.

- ☐ The **PINGUIDITY** of British food tends to put me off. *(n.)*

PINION

(PIN yun) *v.*
to bind the wings so
as not to fly; to confine

Link: **PIN**

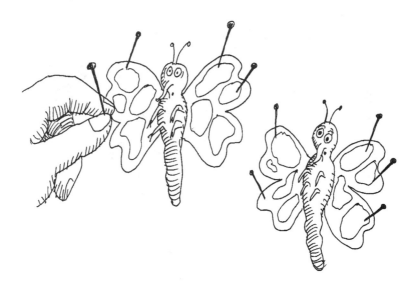

*"The **PINS PINIONED** the butterfly wings."*

- ❑ The handcuffs were used to **PINION** his hands.
- ❑ In order to transport the large bird, the zoo keeper **PINIONED** its wings with soft straps.
- ❑ Jake had **PINIONED** John to the wall before someone could stop the altercation.

PIOUS
(PIE us) *adj.*
devout or virtuous; holy

Link: **PIE**

"A PIOUS PIE"

- ❏ Elizabeth **PIOUSLY** said her prayers every night before bed. *(adv.)*

- ❏ The church was adorned with **PIOUS** artwork from around the world.

- ❏ The opposite of **PIOUS** is **IMPIOUS**, meaning lacking in reverence or respect.

PLETHORA
(PLETH or ah) *n.*
a state of excessive fullness;
superabundance

Link: **FLORA**

*"A **PLETHORA** of **FLORA**"*

☐ There was an awesome **PLETHORA** of food at the picnic.

☐ Jake opened the back door and a **PLETHORA** of mosquitoes flew in.

☐ After placing an ad in the paper to sell my Corvette for $200, I received a **PLETHORA** of calls.

PLIABLE

(PLYE ah bul) *adj.*
receptive to change; easily persuaded
or controlled; easily bent or twisted

Link: **FLY BULL**

*"A **PLIABLE BULL** convinced he can **FLY**."*

- ❑ Students demonstrate their **PLIABILITY** when they remain open to new ideas. *(n.)*

- ❑ Putty is a **PLIABLE** material that can be easily shaped.

- ❑ Bob was always **PLIABLE** to Brenda's demands.

PLUCKY

(PLUCK ee) *adj.*
brave and spirited; courageous

Link: **DUCKY**

*"A **PLUCKY DUCKY**"*

- ❑ He fought his disease in a **PLUCKY** way which we all admired.

- ❑ Her **PLUCKINESS** made her a perfect candidate for the debate team. *(n.)*

- ❑ Because Roger has such a **PLUCKY** attitude, we asked him to be the captain of our sky diving team.

POLARIZE
(POH luh rize) *v.*
to break up into opposing
factions or groups

Link: **POLAR ICE**

*"The Eskimos could not settle their differences
and decided to **POLARIZE** the **POLAR ICE**."*

❑ The issue of what to have for dinner **POLARIZED**
the family; Mom and Sally wanted chicken while
Dad and I wanted steak.

❑ The jury became **POLARIZED** when half thought
the defendant was guilty, and the other half
thought he was innocent.

❑ The football stadium was **POLARIZED** into home
fans occupying the south bleachers and visiting
fans occupying the north bleachers.

POLTROON
(pol TROON) *n.*
a coward

Link: **PLATOON**

*"A **PLATOON** full of **POLTROONS**"*

- ❏ John is usually not scared of anything, but when confronted by a spider he turns into a **POLTROON**.

- ❏ The **POLTROON** always fled when he sensed danger.

- ❏ Many considered him a **POLTROON** because he was in his 30s yet still afraid of the dark.

PORTAL
(POR tul) *n.*
an entrance, door or gate

Link: **PORTHOLE**

"A PORTHOLE PORTAL"

- ❏ As we stepped through the **PORTAL** of the Sistine Chapel, everyone was awestruck.

- ❏ Dante writes about the **PORTALS** of death in his *The Divine Comedy*.

- ❏ The space travelers stepped through the **PORTAL** into another dimension.

Match the word with its definition.

__	1. **philippic**	a.	easily persuaded or controlled
__	2. **pinguid**	b.	devout or virtuous; holy
__	3. **pinion**	c.	brave and spirited; courageous
__	4. **pious**	d.	confine
__	5. **plethora**	e.	a door or gate
__	6. **pliable**	f.	superabundance
__	7. **plucky**	g.	fat
__	8. **polarize**	h.	a verbal denunciation
__	9. **poltroon**	i.	a coward
__	10. **portal**	j.	to break up into opposing groups

Fill in the blanks with the most appropriate word. The word form may need changing.

1. The church was adorned with _____ artwork from around the world.

2. There was an awesome _____ of food at the picnic.

3. The football stadium was _____ into home fans occupying the south bleachers and visiting fans occupying the north bleachers.

4. Mom served a _____ turkey for Thanksgiving dinner.

5. Putty is a _____ material that can be easily shaped.

6. He fought his disease in a _____ way which we all admired.

7. In order to transport the large bird, the zoo keeper _____ its wings with soft straps.

8. John is usually not scared of anything, but when confronted by a spider he turns into a _____.

9. The coach, in seeking to rouse the team, pronounced bitter _____ against the opposing team.

10. As we stepped through the _____ of the Sistine Chapel, everyone was awestruck.

256

PORTEND
(por TEND) *v.*
to warn of as an omen; forecast

Link: **POOR END**

*"His teacher **PORTENDED** that Billy
would come to a **POOR END**."*

- ❑ Black clouds **PORTEND** that a storm is on the way.

- ❑ The Japanese attack on Pearl Harbor **PORTENDED** the United States entering World War II.

- ❑ Banks failures and real estate foreclosures are a few indicators that **PORTEND** a recession.

PRATTLE
(PRAT l) *v.*
to babble; to talk meaninglessly

Link: **RATTLE**

AND MY DEAR, I TOLD OSCAR IF HE'S COMING LATE FOR DINNER HE COULD EAT COLDFROGS FOR ALL I CARED. A POOR HOUSESNAKE WORKS HER RATTLES TO THE BONES AND HER HUSBAND DOESN'T APPRECIATE HER. WHY A MAN WHO DOES THAT IS NO BETTER THAN A SNAKE IN THE GRASS.

"PRATTLING RATTLEsnakes"

- ❑ After Ted awoke from his coma, he began to **PRATTLE** about the accident.

- ❑ The three-year-old **PRATTLED** for hours although no one understood what she was saying.

- ❑ My mother **PRATTLES** so endlessly I barely can understand what she is talking about.

PREDATORY

(PRED ah tor ee) *adj.*
victimizing or destroying others
for one's own gain; pillaging

Link: **BREAD STORY**

"A PREDATORY BREAD STORY"

- ❏ The tiger shark not only looks **PREDATORY**, but is a **PREDATOR**. *(adj./n.)*

- ❏ The killer whale is a **PREDATORY** mammal that is rarely known to harm humans.

- ❏ During the Middle Ages, many **PREDATORY** bands of men roamed England.

PREHENSILE
(pri HEN sil) *adj.*
adapted for grasping or holding

Link: **UTENSIL**

*"The monkey's **PREHENSILE**
tail held the **UTENSIL**."*

- ❏ The elephant uses its **PREHENSILE** trunk the same way humans use their hands.

- ❏ Because of our thumbs, humans are much better at **PREHENSILE** movements than are most other mammals.

- ❏ Monkeys are well adapted for climbing trees because of their **PREHENSILE** tails.

PRESENTIMENT

(pre ZEN tih ment) *n.*
a sense that something is
about to occur; a premonition

Link: **PRESENT**

*"Ted had a **PRESENTIMENT** that
he was not going to like his **PRESENT**."*

❑ Ray had a **PRESENTIMENT** that he would hear
from Tony before the end of the day.

❑ Jane's **PRESENTIMENT** was that one of us would
win an Oscar at the Academy Awards.

❑ The sage had a **PRESENTIMENTAL** vision of an
impending disaster that would befall the village.
(adj.)

PRISTINE

(PRIS teen) *adj.*
extremely pure; untouched

Link: **CLEAN**

*"Marge routinely had her carpets
CLEANED so they would look **PRISTINE**."*

- ❑ The coin discovered under layers of ash was still in **PRISTINE** condition.

- ❑ Those who know about the island keep it a secret because they want to continue to enjoy its **PRISTINE** beaches.

- ❑ When the archeologists discovered the cave, they ascertained that it was **PRISTINE** and that they had been the first to examine it.

PRODIGIOUS
(prah DIJ us) *adj.*
enormous in size, quantity,
degree; marvelous, amazing

Link: **DISH**

SPECIALS
BIG STEAK DISH...$9.95
Chicken Dish 7.95
Fish Dish 8.95
Dish ....

"A PRODIGIOUS DISH"

☐ The construction of the Panama Canal was a
PRODIGIOUS undertaking.

☐ The trainer managed to escape a ferociously
PRODIGIOUS lion by climbing a tree.

☐ The **PRODIGIOUSNESS** of marathon runners
who run twenty-six miles in a few hours is truly
extraordinary. *(n.)*

PROFOUND
(pruh FOUND) *adj.*
intellectually deep or penetrating; reaching to, rising from, or affecting the depths of one's nature

Link: **TOES FOUND**

*"The **TOES** of King Two **TOES** Kahmin was a **PROFOUND** discovery."*

❑ Many psychologists believe violence on television and in film has a **PROFOUND** affect on our behavior toward others.

❑ Advertising has a **PROFOUND** affect on the failure or success of many products.

❑ My professor is a **PROFOUND** thinker.

PROPINQUITY
(proh PING kwi tee) *n.*
proximity, nearness; kinship

Link: **PROXIMITY**

*"The Johnson Twins sit in close **PROXIMITY**
because of their **PROPINQUITY**."*

❏ Because they were in classes together
everyday, a relationship developed based on
PROPINQUITY.

❏ The **PROPINQUITY** of Leonardo di Vinci and
Michelangelo is remarkable; the two great artists
lived at the same time, at the same place.

❏ Because of the **PROPINQUITY** of our neighbor's
yard, we sometimes hear things we shouldn't.

PRUDENT

(PROOD ent) *adj.*
cautious; discreet; exercising
good judgment

Link: **STUDENT**

*"A **PRUDENT STUDENT** prepares
ahead for her math test."*

- ❑ It is always a **PRUDENT** choice not to drink and drive.

- ❑ My mother **PRUDENTLY** guided me through some very difficult times. *(adv.)*

- ❑ Michele decided it would be **PRUDENT** to ignore the insult and to walk away from such a hateful girl.

Match the word with its definition.

__	1. **portend**	a. proximity, nearness; kinship
__	2. **prattle**	b. adapted for grasping or holding
__	3. **predatory**	c. to warn of as an omen; forecast
__	4. **prehensile**	d. a premonition
__	5. **presentiment**	e. extremely pure; untouched
__	6. **pristine**	f. cautious; discreet
__	7. **prodigious**	g. enormous in size or quantity
__	8. **profound**	h. to talk meaninglessly
__	9. **propinquity**	i. pillaging
__	10. **prudent**	j. intellectually deep or penetrating

Fill in the blanks with the most appropriate word. The word form may need changing.

1. Those who know about the island keep it a secret because they want to continue to enjoy its _____ beaches.

2. The killer whale is a _____ mammal that is rarely known to harm humans.

3. The construction of the Panama Canal was a _____ undertaking.

4. Because of the _____ of our neighbor's yard, we sometimes hear things we shouldn't.

5. The elephant uses its _____ trunk the same way humans use their hands.

6. It is always a _____ choice not to drink and drive.

7. After Ted awoke from his coma, he began to _____ about the accident.

8. Many psychologists believe violence on television and in film has a _____ affect on our behavior toward others.

9. Ray had a _____ that he would hear from Tony before the end of the day.

10. Black clouds _____ that a storm is on the way.

PSYCHE
(SYE kee) *n.*
the human soul; the mind

Link: **BIKE**

"The PSYCHE of a BIKE lover"

- ❑ The study of poetry often helps students to examine their own **PSYCHE**.

- ❑ Because the inmate was so hardened in crime, it was difficult to imagine that he possessed a **PSYCHE**.

- ❑ A true appreciation for classical literature engages one's **PSYCHE**.

PURBLIND

(PUR blind) *adj.*
having poor vision;
nearly or partly blind

Link: **PURR BLIND**

*"The **PURBLIND** cat **PURRED** as it
was led by its seeing-eye mouse."*

❑ I am afraid that when it comes to mathematics, I am **PURBLIND**.

❑ The **PURBLIND** man was undergoing surgery to restore his sight.

❑ The bright flashes of light from the cameras made the actor temporarily **PURBLIND**.

QUAFF
(kwaf) *v.*
to drink heartily

Link: **GIRAFFE**

*"A **QUAFFING GIRAFFE**"*

- ❑ I offered her a sip, but she **QUAFFED** my entire soda.

- ❑ Fraternity parties often involve the **QUAFFING** of large quantities of beverages.

- ❑ Many of the senior citizens were guilty of **QUAFFING** far too much drink at the early bird special.

QUAIL

(kwayl) *v.*
to shrink with fear; to cower;
to lose heart and courage

Link: **QUAIL (bird)**

"A QUAILING QUAIL"

- ❏ The quarterback did not **QUAIL** as the defensive line ran to crush him.

- ❏ A leader is one who does not **QUAIL** in the face of adversity.

- ❏ The previously beaten dog **QUAILED** each time his new owner raised his hand.

QUELL

(kwel) *v.*
to extinguish; to put down
or suppress by force

Link: **QUILT**

*"Grandma **QUELLED** the fire with a **QUILT**."*

- ❑ The mother attempted to **QUELL** the infant's cries by singing a lullaby.

- ❑ The National Guard was sent in to try to **QUELL** the rioting crowd.

- ❑ A mob stabbed Caesar in an attempt to **QUELL** his power.

QUIETUDE
(KWIE ih tude) *n.*
calm; tranquility; peacefulness

Link: **QUIET DUDE**

*"Dad was a **QUIET DUDE**
who sought **QUIETUDE**."*

- ❑ Gene and Chris chose their property for the air of **QUIETUDE** and peace that pervaded the area.

- ❑ After the long illness, he had finally found **QUIETUDE** in death.

- ❑ The **QUIETUDE** of the substitute teacher took the whole class by surprise.

RAFFISH
(RAF ish) *adj.*
cheaply vulgar in appearance or
nature; tawdry; disreputable

Link: **FISH**

"A RAFFISH FISH"

- ❑ The **RAFFISH** character had been seen at the scene of the murder and was taken in for questioning.

- ❑ Pete's parents were shocked to see the **RAFFISH** living conditions of his college dorm.

- ❑ Because of his **RAFFISHNESS**, the authorities escorted him from the stadium. *(n.)*

RANSACK
(RAN sak) *v.*
to search thoroughly; pillage

Link: **RAN SACK**

*"The police **RAN** in **SACKS** to **RANSACK**
the suspect's apartment."*

- ❏ April was late for school and **RANSACKED** her room in order to find her car keys.

- ❏ The thieves not only broke in, but they also **RANSACKED** the office looking for valuables.

- ❏ The king and his men were busy **RANSACKING** the village and did not know a truce had been called.

REIGN

(rayn) *n.*
the exercise or possession
of supreme power

Link: **RAIN**

*"Frogs **REIGN** in the **RAIN**."*

❑ Queen Elizabeth has **REIGNED** over England
   since the 1950s.

❑ Many believe the king's **REIGN** was strikingly
   enlightened.

❑ The new winner of the Miss America pageant
   began her **REIGN** by taking the crown of last
   year's winner.

REPLETE

(rih PLEET) *adj.*
full or supplied to the utmost; gorged

Link: **PETE**

*"**PETE** was **REPLETE** with
supplies for his camping trip."*

- ❑ We ordered our pizza with "the works"; it was **REPLETE** with sausage, ham, pepperoni, olives, onions, and anchovies.

- ❑ Craig was well prepared for his fishing trip; his **REPLETE** tackle box had every kind of lure.

- ❑ The **REPLETE** buffet had many tantalizing dishes.

Match the word with its definition.

___ 1.	**psyche**	a.	having poor vision
___ 2.	**purblind**	b.	to put down or suppress by force
___ 3.	**quaff**	c.	the possession of supreme power
___ 4.	**quail**	d.	to shrink with fear
___ 5.	**quell**	e.	full or supplied to the utmost; gorge
___ 6.	**quietude**	f.	the human soul; the mind
___ 7.	**raffish**	g.	to search thoroughly; pillage
___ 8.	**ransack**	h.	cheaply vulgar in appearance
___ 9.	**reign**	i.	calm; tranquility; peacefulness
___ 10.	**replete**	j.	to drink heartily

Fill in the blanks with the most appropriate word. The word form may need changing.

1. The quarterback did not _____ as the defensive line ran to crush him.

2. The National Guard was sent in to try to _____ the rioting crowd.

3. After the long illness, he had finally found _____ in death.

4. Queen Elizabeth has _____ over England since the 1950's.

5. The _____ man was undergoing surgery to restore his sight.

6. I offered her a sip, but she _____ my entire soda.

7. A true appreciation for classical literature engages one's _____.

8. Craig was well prepared for his fishing trip; his _____ tackle box had every kind of lure.

9. April was late for school and _____ her room in order to find her car keys.

10. Pete's parents were shocked to see the _____ living conditions of his college dorm.

278

REPROACH

(rih PROACH) *v./n.*
to express disapproval of; an
expression of disapproval

Link: **COACH**

*"The **COACH REPROACHED** his players." (adj.)*

❑ Jessica's teacher wrote a recommendation for her because her work had always been above **REPROACH**. *(n.)*

❑ The mother **REPROACHED** her daughter for not cleaning her room. *(v.)*

❑ Although he realized his behavior was not beyond **REPROACH**, he didn't think it was bad enough for him to be suspended from school. *(n.)*

REQUISITE
(REK kwuh zit) *n.*
essential; necessary

Link: **WRECK SIT**

*"It's not **REQUISITE** to **SIT** on the
WRECK until the police arrive."*

- ❑ On the first day of class the teacher explained
  that doing our homework is not only important, it
  is **REQUISITE**.

- ❑ Successfully completing Latin I is **REQUISITE** to
  taking Latin II.

- ❑ This movie is a **REQUISITE** for movie buffs.

RESPITE
(RES pit) *n.*
delay; postpone; a brief
interval of rest

Link: **REST A BIT**

*"After pitching a double header, David
took a **RESPITE** to **REST A BIT**."*

❑ The condemned man was given a **RESPITE** to
enjoy his favorite meal before his execution.

❑ The class had worked so hard throughout the
semester that the teacher gave them a **RESPITE**
before their exam.

❑ The hikers enjoyed a much needed **RESPITE**
after hiking for two hours on the arduous trail.

RHETORIC

(RET or ik) *n.*
the art or study of using language effectively
and persuasively; over-elaborate language

Link: **RENT-A-WRECK**

*"A salesman's **RENT-A-WRECK RHETORIC**"*

- ❏ Famous sportscaster, Howard Cosell, is well
  known for his **RHETORICAL** sports analysis.
  (adj.)

- ❏ The politician's speech was mostly **RHETORIC**
  and lip service.

- ❏ William Cullen Bryant was a master of
  RHETORIC and one of our country's most
  famous editors.

RIFE

(ryfe) *adj.*
abundant; great in number or amount

Link: **LIFE**

*"The ocean is **RIFE** with **LIFE**."*

- ❏ The new, tough administrator was sent to take over the hospital which was **RIFE** with problems.

- ❏ When I got my paper back, it was covered with red ink; the teacher said it was **RIFE** with errors.

- ❏ Brad's dorm was **RIFE** with cockroaches.

ROTE

(roht) *n.*

a memorizing process using routine or repetition, often without comprehension; learned or memorized by rote

Link: **ROPE**

"ROTE ROPING"

❑ Foreign languages are no longer taught by **ROTE**.

❑ Although Allison had not been in a church for years, by **ROTE** she knew how to do everything correctly.

❑ Learning vocabulary by **ROTE** may help you pass a test in the short term, but may not be effective in the long term.

RUMINATE

(ROO mih nate) *n.*
to ponder; to reflect upon

Link: **ROOMMATE**

*"Larry didn't have to **RUMINATE** about taking this guy as a **ROOMMATE**."*

❑ Because she had made up her mind, Nancy did not need time to **RUMINATE** when Pete asked her to marry him.

❑ Sitting in detention, Scott had plenty of time to **RUMINATE** about what his parents were going to say when he got home.

❑ Michael often **RUMINATED** about the day when his horse would win the Kentucky Derby.

SAGA
(SAH gah) *n.*
a long story, often telling
the history of a family

Link: **GAGA**

*"A **GAGA SAGA**"*

- ☐ The **SAGA** of Odysseus has been retold throughout history.

- ☐ I thought Jennifer wanted to tell me about her argument with her mother, but after twenty minutes I could see it was turning into a **SAGA**.

- ☐ *Moby Dick* is a **SAGA** of the sea written by Herman Melville.

SAGE

(sayj) *n.*
a person of wisdom and prudence;
wise through reflection and experience

Link: **PAGE**

*"A **SAGE** reads each **PAGE**."*

- During ancient times a **SAGE** was consulted for momentous decisions.

- Native American tribes regarded their medicine man as a **SAGE** with special healing powers.

- In our family we consider our grandparents the **SAGES** of the family.

SCRUPULOUS
(SKROO pyu les) *adj.*
careful of small details; honest; conscientious

Link: **SCREWS**

*"Aircraft manufacturers must be **SCRUPULOUS**
with the placement of **SCREWS**."*

❑ Because his parents are such **SCRUPULOUS**
people, Jim knew the difference between right and
wrong even as a small boy.

❑ President Abraham Lincoln is known for his
SCRUPULOUSNESS. *(n.)*

❑ The clerk **SCRUPULOUSLY** followed the man to
his car to give him the change he had forgotten.
(adv.)

VOCABULARY CARTOONS Review #25

Match the word with its definition.

___ 1. **reproach**   a. great in number or amount
___ 2. **requisite**   b. essential; necessary
___ 3. **respite**   c. a memorizing process using repetition
___ 4. **rhetoric**   d. to ponder; to reflect upon
___ 5. **rife**   e. to express disapproval of
___ 6. **rote**   f. a person of wisdom and prudence
___ 7. **ruminate**   g. a story of the history of a family
___ 8. **saga**   h. over-elaborate language
___ 9. **sage**   i. careful of small details; honest
___ 10. **scrupulous**   j. a brief interval of rest

Fill in the blanks with the most appropriate word. The word form may need changing.

1. Brad's dorm was _____ with cockroaches.

2. Learning vocabulary by _____ memory my help you pass a test in the short term, but may not be effective in the long term.

3. The mother _____ her daughter for not cleaning her room.

4. Sitting in detention, Scott had plenty of time to _____ about what his parents were going to say when he got home.

5. On the first day of class the teacher explained that doing our homework is not only important, it is _____.

6. The hikers enjoyed a much needed _____ after hiking for two hours on the arduous trail.

7. In our family we consider our grandparents the _____ of the family.

8. Because his parents are such _____ people, Jim knew the difference between right and wrong even as a small boy.

9. The politician's speech was mostly _____ and lip service.

10. The _____ of Odysseus has been retold throughout history.

SEDENTARY

(SED en ter ee) *adj.*
characterized by or requiring much
sitting; accustomed to little exercise

Link: **SIT AND STARE**

*"**SEDENTARY** Larry often would **SIT AND STARE**."*

- ❑ "A **SEDENTARY** lifestyle can lead to heart problems," the doctor explained as he urged the patient to exercise regularly.

- ❑ Because of a stroke, the normally active woman was forced to lead a more **SEDENTARY** life.

- ❑ The **SEDENTARY** nature of a secretary's job would make it impractical for a restless person.

SEETHE

(seeth) *v.*
to be agitated, as by rage; to
churn and foam as if boiling

Link: **TEETHE**

*"Babies **SEETHE** when they **TEETHE**."*

❑ The class watched the **SEETHING** teacher take a
deep breath before she reprimanded the student.

❑ When he learned that his kingdom had been
conquered, the king **SEETHED** with anger.

❑ I could see my father start to **SEETHE** as he read
the phone bill.

SERENE

(suh REEN) *adj.*
clear; calm; tranquil

Link: **SCENE**

*"Teachers often daydream
of a SERENE SCENE."*

- ☐ The *Mona Lisa* has a **SERENE** smile.
- ☐ Game day dawned with a **SERENE** sky.
- ☐ The highlight of our cruise is when we snorkeled in the **SERENE** waters of the Cayman Islands.

SHUNT

(shunt) *v.*
to move or turn aside; to evade
by putting aside or ignoring

Link: **RUNT**

*"The mother dog **SHUNTING** the **RUNT** of the litter"*

❑ The crash was caused by failure of the engineer
to **SHUNT** the train onto the proper rails.

❑ After smoking for twenty nine years, Larry found it
hard to **SHUNT** his bad habit.

❑ The running back dashed down the field
SHUNTING right and left to avoid the tacklers.

SKULLDUGGERY
(skul DUG uh ree) *n.*
trickery; underhandedness

Link: **SKULL DUG**

*"Young Indiana Jones was
up to some **SKULLDUGGERY**."*

❏ The charlatan was guilty of **SKULLDUGGERY**.

❏ In order to capture ships at sea, pirates would practice all types of **SKULLDUGGERY** to gain an advantage over their prey.

❏ After his arrest, he admitted to numerous counts of **SKULLDUGGERY** that had plagued his town for years.

SLAKE

(slayk) *v.*
to quench; to satisfy a craving

Link: **LAKE**

*"Larry **SLAKED** his thirst in the **LAKE**."*

- During halftime, the quarterback tried to **SLAKE** his thirst by drinking Gatorade.

- Ben read everything he could in an attempt to **SLAKE** his desire for knowledge.

- Jeannie **SLAKED** her nicotine craving by going outdoors to have a cigarette.

SPAWN
(spahn) *v.*
to give rise to; to produce
in large numbers

Link: **YAWN**

"A SPAWNED YAWN"

- Salmon always return to their native streams to **SPAWN**.

- Joe's negative outlook **SPAWNED** hard feelings in his teammates.

- The flu outbreak **SPAWNED** major attendance problems at the school.

SPECTER
(SPEK ter) *n.*
a ghost or phantom

Link: **SPECTACLES**

*"A **SPECTER** with **SPECTACLES**"*

- After the kids yelled "trick or treat," a **SPECTER** appeared in the door causing them to run away without getting any candy.

- As the lights came up on stage, a **SPECTER** seemed to materialize from nowhere.

- We ran from the house after we saw a **SPECTER** come down the staircase.

SPURIOUS
(SPUR ee us) *adj.*
not genuine; false

"SPURIOUS SPURS"

- ❑ The politician made **SPURIOUS** claims about his opponent's views of labor reform.

- ❑ The police discovered cheap items which were carrying expensive labels being **SPURIOUSLY** manufactured in an illegal operation in the city. *(adv.)*

- ❑ An expert was called in to examine the antiques for **SPURIOUSNESS**. *(n.)*

SQUALID
(SQUAW lid) *adj.*
dirty and wretched, as
from poverty or lack of care

Link: **SQUID**

*"A **SQUALID SQUID**"*

❑ The house was completely run down; it was
   amazing how someone could live in such
   SQUALID conditions.

❑ After the old recluse had died, animal lovers
   made their way through the **SQUALIDITY** of her
   home as they rescued eighty cats. *(n.)*

❑ Upton Sinclair wrote about the **SQUALID** life of
   the meat packers in Chicago during the early
   1900s.

Match the word with its definition.

___	1. **sedentary**	a.	clear; calm; tranquil
___	2. **seethe**	b.	to quench; to satisfy a craving
___	3. **serene**	c.	dirty and wretched
___	4. **shunt**	d.	requiring much sitting
___	5. **skullduggery**	e.	not genuine; false
___	6. **slake**	f.	a ghost or phantom
___	7. **spawn**	g.	to give rise to
___	8. **specter**	h.	to be agitated, as by rage
___	9. **spurious**	i.	trickery; underhandedness
___	10. **squalid**	j.	to evade by putting aside or ignoring

Fill in the blanks with the most appropriate word. The word form may need changing.

1. After smoking for twenty nine years, Larry found it hard to _____ his bad habit.

2. During halftime, the quarterback tried to _____ his thirst by drinking Gatorade.

3. I could see my father start to _____ as he read the phone bill.

4. Because of a stroke, the normally active woman was forced to lead a more _____ life.

5. Joe's negative outlook _____ hard feelings in his teammates.

6. The highlight of our cruise is when we snorkeled in the _____ waters of the Cayman Islands.

7. The charlatan was guilty of _____.

8. The politician made _____ claims about his opponent's views of labor reform.

9. After the kids yelled "trick or treat," a _____ appeared in the door causing them to run away without getting any candy.

10. The house was completely run down; it was amazing how someone could live in such _____ conditions.

STALACTITE

(stah LAK tite) *n.*
a tapering formation hanging from
the ceiling of a cave, produced by the
dripping of mineral-rich water

Link: **TIGHTS**

*"**STALACTITES** hang down
like her loose **TIGHTS**."*

- ❑ As we worked ourselves through the cave we had
  to be aware of **STALACTITES** so we wouldn't
  bump our heads.

- ❑ The icicle looked like a giant **STALACTITE** as it
  grew drip by drip during the winter.

- ❑ Another way to remember **STALACTITE** is: A
  STALACTITE has to hold **TIGHT** to the ceiling so
  it won't fall.

STALAGMITE

(stah LAG mite) *n.*
a conical mineral deposit formed
on the floor of a cave by the
dripping of mineral-rich water

Link: **MITES**

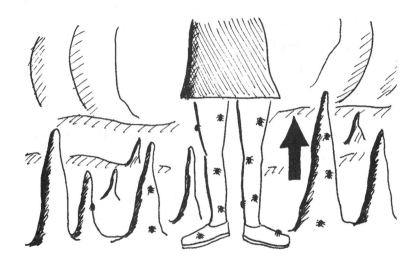

*"The **MITES** climb up the **STALAGMITES**."*

- ❏ The **STALAGMITE** grew straight up in the center of the cave.

- ❏ While exploring the cave, I tripped over a huge **STALAGMITE**.

- ❏ It is hard to believe that a giant **STALAGMITE** was once just a lump on the cave's floor.

STRIFE
(stryfe) *n.*
bitter conflict; quarrel; fight

Link: **LIFE**

*"There was little **STRIFE** in Amanda's **LIFE**."*

❏ He was thin and gaunt and had led a life full of **STRIFE**.

❏ It was a time of great **STRIFE** in the kingdom because of three seasons of failed crops.

❏ A life of poverty is filled with much **STRIFE**.

SUBLIME
(suh BLYME) *adj.*
impressive; inspiring awe; majestic

Link: **SUB LIME**

*"The Navy's new **SUB LIME**
was **SUBLIME**."*

- ❑ The lecturer had something to offer each of his listeners; he was a master of moving his speech from the ridiculous to the **SUBLIME**.

- ❑ The **SUBLIME** melody worked itself throughout the entire musical.

- ❑ The priest's **SUBLIME** voice made him the object of admiration in his parish.

SUCCINCT

(suhk SINGKT) *adj.*
brief and to the point;
concise and terse

Link: **SINK**

*"Virginia was **SUCCINCT** when
Ernie forgot to fix the **SINK**."*

❑ When Joe was called upon, he **SUCCINCTLY**
paraphrased what the teacher had just explained.
(adv.)

❑ The policeman asked the witnesses to be
SUCCINCT in recounting what they saw.

❑ The mother's reprimand was **SUCCINCT** but
effective.

SUPINE
(SUE pine) *adj.*
lying on the back with the face
turned upward; inclined

Link: **SPINE**

*"Lying **SUPINE** on the **SPINE**"*

- ❑ When the investigators arrived, the body was **SUPINE** in the middle of the living room floor.

- ❑ The chiropractor had Jill lie in a **SUPINE** position so he could adjust her neck.

- ❑ The referee stopped the fight when the boxer lay on the mat in a **SUPINE** position and could not get up.

SURMISE
(sur MIZE) *v.*
to guess; to infer (something)
without sufficient evidence

Link: **SUNRISE**

*"Run for cover, I **SURMISE** a **SUNRISE**!"*

❑ The detective was able to **SURMISE** the identity
of the murderer by the clues left behind.

❑ When everyone began to laugh, I **SURMISED** that
I had been the butt of a practical joke.

❑ Beginning with the very first date, Liz is good at
SURMISING how a relationship will turn out.

SURREPTITIOUS
(sur ep TISH us) *adj.*
done or acting in a secret, sly manner

Link: **SUSPICIOUS**

"To escape from the circus, an elephant has to be
***SURREPTITIOUS** without being **SUSPICIOUS**."*

- ❏ The **SURREPTITOUS** lion stalked its prey from behind the tall grass.

- ❏ Helen **SURREPTITIOUSLY** crept around the car, hoping to get the cat out from under it. *(adv.)*

- ❏ The magician was so **SURREPTITIOUS** during his magic trick that the audience was completely fooled.

Link: **FELT**

*"Tina **FELT** great when she became **SVELTE**."*

- ❑ The ballerina appeared as **SVELTE** as an angel as she floated effortlessly across the stage.

- ❑ One way to stay **SVELTE** is to exercise and eat right.

- ❑ The **SVELTE** waitress was able to move easily between the closely arranged tables.

SYMMETRY

(SIM ih tree) *n.*
exact correspondence of form on
opposite sides of a dividing line

Link: **CEMETERY**

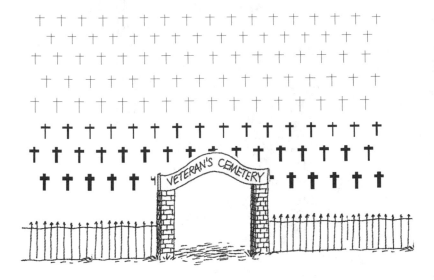

"SYMMETRY in the CEMETERY"

- ❑ The **SYMMETRY** of the garden added to its beauty.

- ❑ The **SYMMETRY** of the Golden Gate Bridge is an awesome sight.

- ❑ The dancers' **SYMMETRY** required lots of practice to perfect.

VOCABULARY CARTOONS Review #27

___	1. **stalactite**	a. to guess
___	2. **stalagmite**	b. slim, slender
___	3. **strife**	c. brief and to the point
___	4. **sublime**	d. bitter conflict; quarrel; fight
___	5. **succinct**	e. sly in manner
___	6. **supine**	f. lying on the back
___	7. **surmise**	g. a hanging formation in a cave
___	8. **surreptitious**	h. exact correspondence of form
___	9. **svelte**	i. impressive; inspiring awe; majestic
___	10. **symmetry**	j. a formation rising from the floor of a cave

Fill in the blanks with the most appropriate word. The word form may need changing.

1. The priest's _____ voice made him the object of admiration in his parish.

2. When the investigators arrived, the body was _____ in the middle of the living room floor.

3. The detective was able to _____ the identity of the murderer by the clues left behind.

4. He was thin and gaunt and had led a life full of _____.

5. One way to stay _____ is to exercise and eat right.

6. While exploring the cave, I tripped over a huge _____ .

7. As we worked ourselves through the cave we had to be aware of _____ so we wouldn't bump our heads.

8. The _____ of the Golden Gate Bridge is an awesome sight.

9. The policeman asked the witnesses to be _____ in recounting what they saw.

10. The _____ lion stalked its prey from behind the tall grass.

SYNCHRONIZE
(SING kra nize) *v.*
to occur at the same time; simultaneous

Link: **SINK**

*"The commandos **SYNCHRONIZED** their **SINKS**."*

❑ **SYNCHRONIZED** swimming is entertaining to watch. *(adj.)*

❑ The captain had his troops **SYNCHRONIZE** their watches in order to begin the attack at the same time.

❑ One of the jobs of a film editor is to **SYNCHRONIZE** the stunts so the audience cannot detect where the stuntman took over.

TANTALIZE

(TAN tul ize) *v.*
to excite by exposing something desirable
while keeping it out of reach: to tease

Link: **SANTA'S LIES**

I'M SANTA. I LIVE IN THE NORTH POLE. I CAME HERE WITH MY REINDEER. I COME DOWN THE CHIMNEY ON XMAS.

"SANTA'S LIES TANTALIZE."

❏ The **TANTALIZING** aroma of the bread made us all very hungry. *(adj.)*

❏ Jessica would **TANTALIZE** all the boys with her beauty but would never accept a date.

❏ Although the prospect of extra money was **TANTALIZING**, Joe refused to break the law to get it. *(adj.)*

TAUT

(tawt) *adj.*
stretched tight; tidy

Link: **CAUGHT**

*"Eric **CAUGHT** a lot of fish
because his line was **TAUT**."*

❏ The sailor pulled the lines **TAUT**, so he could sail against the wind.

❏ As he stared down the snout of the bull, the toreador's muscles became as **TAUT** as piano wire.

❏ The commander was proud that he ran such a **TAUT** ship.

TAWDRY
(TAW dree) *adj.*
gaudy and cheap in appearance or nature

Link: **AUDREY**

"TAWDRY AUDREY"

- ❑ Scott gave Rhonda a **TAWDRY** engagement ring and could tell by her face that she didn't like it.

- ❑ Shirley's **TAWDRY** dress was the talk of all the gossips.

- ❑ The innocent children believed the **TAWDRY** jewels in their mother's bureau were worth a fortune.

TENACIOUS

(teh NAY shus) *adj.*
tough; stubborn; not letting go

Link: **TENNIS ACES**

"TENNIS ACES are TENACIOUS."

- ☐ The fisherman finally landed the **TENACIOUS** marlin after a three and a half hour fight.

- ☐ Susan's **TENACIOUS** efforts to learn English won her the admiration of her teacher.

- ☐ We had no luck eradicating the **TENACIOUS** weeds in our front lawn.

TERSE
(turs) *adj.*
brief and to the point; concise

Link: **VERSE**

"A TERSE VERSE"

- Rich could tell he had annoyed his teacher when she gave him a **TERSE** reply.

- Hemingway is best known for his **TERSE** style of writing.

- When Sally becomes annoyed and wants to make her point, she becomes very **TERSE**.

THRONG

(throng) *n./v.*
a large group of people gathered
closely together; to crowd upon

Link: **SONG**

*"The **THRONG** broke into **SONG**."* *(n.)*

❑ When the Pope visited the United States, an
   admiring **THRONG** gathered at every major city.
   (n.)

❑ A **THRONG** of revelers gather at Times Square
   in New York City on New Year's Eve. *(n.)*

❑ The assassins **THRONGED** around Caesar
   before they murdered him. *(v.)*

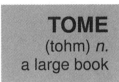

TOME
(tohm) *n.*
a large book

Link: **HOME**

*"A bookworm's **HOME** is a **TOME**."*

- ❏ The witch pulled a **TOME** from the shelf and looked for a spell.

- ❏ Thank goodness encyclopedias are now on CD-rom so we don't have to find room for all those **TOMES** in our house.

- ❏ The professor carried the Shakespearean **TOME** as if it were a Bible.

TORPID

(TOR pid) *adj.*
dormant; inactive; lethargic

Link: **TORPEDO**

"TORPID TORPEDOES"

❑ The teacher could not understand the boy's **TORPID** reactions until she learned that he could not understand English.

❑ During winter, bears sleep **TORPIDLY** in caves. *(adv.)*

❑ Volcanoes may be **TORPID** for centuries and one day suddenly erupt.

TORRID

(TOR id) *adj.*
intensely hot; burning;
passionate; rapid

Link: **POOR ED**

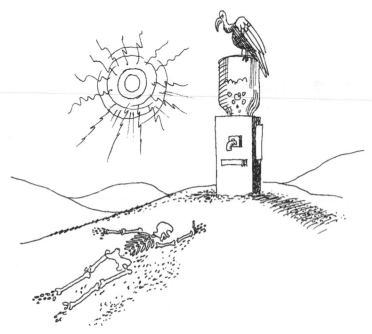

*"**POOR ED** never survived the **TORRID** desert."*

❑ The **TORRID** heat and wind are what led to the Dust Bowl of the 1930s.

❑ Many romance novels contain **TORRID** love affairs.

❑ The salesman **TORRIDLY** spoke to the group hoping to sell them a time share in paradise. *(adv.)*

VOCABULARY CARTOONS Review #28

Match the word with its definition.

___ 1. **synchronize**	a. a large book
___ 2. **tantalize**	b. to occur at the same time
___ 3. **taut**	c. a large group of people
___ 4. **tawdry**	d. dormant; inactive; lethargic
___ 5. **tenacious**	e. stretched tight; tidy
___ 6. **terse**	f. intensely hot; burning
___ 7. **throng**	g. tough; stubborn; not letting go
___ 8. **tome**	h. to tease
___ 9. **torpid**	i. gaudy and cheap
___ 10. **torrid**	j. brief and to the point; concise

Fill in the blanks with the most appropriate word.
The word form may need changing.

1. We had no luck eradicating the _____ weeds in our front lawn.

2. A _____ of revelers gather at Times Square in New York City on New Year's Eve.

3. Rich could tell he had annoyed his teacher when she gave him a _____ reply.

4. Scott gave Rhonda a _____ engagement ring and could tell by her face that she didn't like it.

5. The witch pulled a _____ from the shelf and looked for a spell.

6. The _____ heat and wind are what led to the Dust Bowl of the 1930s.

7. The _____ aroma of the bread made us all very hungry.

8. The captain had his troops _____ their watches in order to begin the attack at the same time.

9. The commander was proud that he ran such a _____ ship.

10. Volcanoes may be _____ for centuries and one day suddenly erupt.

TRAVAIL
(truh VAYL) *n.*
strenuous physical or mental labor
or effort; the labor of childbirth

Link: **TRAIL**

*"Much **TRAVAIL** was required
crossing the Oregon **TRAIL**."*

- ❑ Modern medicine has helped lessen the **TRAVAIL** of childbirth.

- ❑ When he saw his flourishing crops, he realized his **TRAVAIL** had been worth it.

- ❑ Her face showed the lines of her **TRAVAIL** with cancer.

VALIDATE

(VAL ih dayt) *v.*
to declare legally valid; legalize

Link: **VAL'S DATE**

*"Ken **VALIDATED** himself as **VAL'S DATE**."*

❑ The couple decided to marry and **VALIDATE** their relationship.

❑ The award gave Sue a sense of **VALIDATION** that her work was important. *(n.)*

❑ The parking ticket had to be **VALIDATED** by one of the merchants.

VENT

(vent) *n./v.*
a means of escape or release;
an outlet; a small hole; to release

Link: **VENT**

*"Professor Jones **VENTING** his frustration" (v.)*

- ❑ George felt the need to **VENT** his anger in class even if it resulted in suspension. *(v.)*

- ❑ As the boys searched the coastline, they found a **VENT** in which they could hide. *(n.)*

- ❑ At the funeral everyone gave **VENT** to their emotions by openly weeping. *(v.)*

VORACIOUS

(vo RAY shus) *adj.*
an insatiable appetite for an activity or pursuit;
eager to consume great amounts of food

Link: **GOOD GRACIOUS**

*"**GOOD GRACIOUS**, what **VORACIOUS** fish."*

- ❏ The dog's **VORACIOUS** appetite could not be satisfied with small treats.

- ❏ Piranha are **VORACIOUS** carnivores.

- ❏ Teenage boys tend to be **VORACIOUS** eaters.

WAFFLE
(WOF ul) *v.*
to speak or write evasively

Link: **WAFFLE**

*"A **WAFFLE WAFFLING** on the questions."*

❑ When asked by the journalist if he felt he was deserving of the Oscar, the actor **WAFFLED** on his reply since he knew he had done very little real acting.

❑ The president knew he would need to **WAFFLE** on some of the questions the press would ask about the scandal surrounding his administration.

❑ Speech writers make a living **WAFFLING** on the issues.

WINCE

(wints) *v.*
to flinch; to shrink back or start
aside, as from a blow or pain

Link: **PRINCE**

*"The **PRINCE WINCED** when he
slipped on Cinderella's glass slipper."*

- ❑ When she saw her test score, she **WINCED** at the thought of having to show it to her parents.

- ❑ Certain sounds, like the scratching of fingernails on chalk boards, seem to make most people **WINCE**.

- ❑ The puppy **WINCED** when the man tried to pet it.

Link: **MINNOW**

*"They **WINNOWED** the **MINNOWS**."*

❑ The proofreader **WINNOWED** all the grammatical errors in the article before it went to press.

❑ When the children were allowed to choose their own groups, a natural **WINNOWING** occurred.

❑ The wild dogs **WINNOWED** the offal, trying to get some nutrition.

WRATH
(rath) *n.*
extreme or violent rage

Link: **RATS**

*"Monica revealing her **WRATH** for **RATS**"*

- ❑ The Puritans feared the **WRATH** of God above all else.

- ❑ After she had been caught cheating, Judi awaited the **WRATH** of the assistant principal.

- ❑ Her eyes were full of **WRATH** as she glared at his new girlfriend.

WRITHE
(ryth) *v.*
to cause to twist or bend; to suffer
acutely, as in pain or embarrassment

Link: **RIDE**

*"Wild horses **WRITHE** when cowboys **RIDE**."*

- ❏ The fish **WRITHED** free of the hook and escaped back into the sea.

- ❏ Some forms of dance make it look as though the dancer is **WRITHING** in pain.

- ❏ Tina **WRITHED** when the class heard she had failed chemistry for the third time.

ZENITH
(ZEE nith) *n.*
the peak; the highest point

Link: **BENEATH IT**

*"When the Sun is at its **ZENITH**,
you are directly **BENEATH IT**."*

- ❑ The sun reached its **ZENITH** at noon.

- ❑ Nick Faldo claimed that winning The Masters Tournament was the **ZENITH** of his golfing career.

- ❑ After the whale broke the water, he reached his **ZENITH** before he started his descent.
